Bullets and Bosses Don't Have Friends

Toni Crowe

Copyright © 2020
ISBN: 978-1-950216-01-7

Toni Crowe All rights reserved. No part of this publication may be reproduced, distributed, or transmitted in any form or by any means, including photocopying, recording, or other electronic or mechanical methods, without the prior written permission of the publisher except in the case of brief quotations embodied in reviews and certain other non-commercial uses permitted by copyright law.

Editing: Nerdy WordSmith
Cover Art: Nina Z
Formatting: Polgarus Studio

Thank you for purchasing my book "Bullets and Bosses Don't Have Friends, How to Navigate Tough Challenges in the Workplace, My Journey Book 3".

As a thank you gift, I am giving away follow-on short story of my debut autobiography "Where is Baby?" which details the rest of the life of Baby, one of the escorts I lived with when I lived in Cleveland.

https://www.tonicrowewriter.com/thank-you-for-reading-my-book-back-page/

Authors' Note

Bullets and Bosses Don't Have Friends: How to Navigate Tough Challenges in the Workplace is book three of my four book, $7 series. *Bullets and Bosses Don't Have Friends* is an account of my real-life experiences with terrible bosses as I climbed the ladder of success in corporate America. I ended my career as Vice President of Operations in a division of a $1.2B UK company. At the height of my responsibility, I oversaw 3,000 people in two divisions worth $460M.

It would do no good to identify the companies where I worked or the individual managers, Directors, Vice Presidents, Presidents, and CEO's who misbehaved. Bad leaders exist in every corporation. They cannot be avoided. I have therefore deliberately disguised every company and every boss.

I do provide the position I held when each experience happened. I also offer the type of company, as that is essential information associated with the behavior of the leaders.

I made some mistakes in my career that I should have avoided. My ignorance of the written and unwritten rules of corporate America was stunning. I knew no one who had risen higher than assembler. Just as I was the first person in my family to graduate from college, I was the first to be promoted up the ladder.

There is no need for others to repeat my mistakes. Some of these experiences are relatively amusing in hindsight, but let me assure you, they were not funny when I experienced them. I am glad that we can laugh at them together now.

There are three people who loved me unconditionally as I grew into a woman: my mother, Natalie Crowe; my dad, Benjamin Kermit Crowe; and my grandmother, Vandella Dickson. Having unconditional love allowed me to make mistakes and be forgiven. I miss their love.

Myself

I have to live with myself and so
I want to be fit for myself to know.
I want to be able as days go by,
always to look myself straight in the eye;
I don't want to stand with the setting sun
and hate myself for the things I have done.
I don't want to keep on a closet shelf
a lot of secrets about myself
and fool myself as I come and go
into thinking no one else will ever know
the kind of person I really am,
I don't want to dress up myself in sham.
I want to go out with my head erect
I want to deserve all men's respect;
but here in the struggle for fame and wealth
I want to be able to like myself.
I don't want to look at myself and know that
I am bluster and bluff and empty show.
I never can hide myself from me;
I see what others may never see;
I know what others may never know,
I never can fool myself and so,
whatever happens I want to be
self-respecting and conscience free

Edgar Guest, 1881–1959

Contents

1. The Corporate World 1
2. Fit in to Get in 9
3. Protect Your Team 14
4. Working for a Toxic Boss 18
5. Dick in His Hand 26
6. Be an Expert 32
7. Know the Unwritten Rules 37
8. If You Are Leaving, Leave 40
9. Understand Your Environment 45
10. Golden Boys 50
11. Who Is Your Customer? 56
12. WTF? 62
13. Cheater 67
14. Demoted Boss 71
15. Get It in Writing 74
16. Don't Write Checks You Can't Cash 79
17. Don't Tell Them You Are Leaving 84
18. Dead or Alive 87
19. Treachery 90
20. Read and Understand the Contract 95
21. Putting It All to Use 99

Excerpt: Never A $7 Wh*re	103
Acknowledgments	113
Appendix A Citations	117
Appendix B Promotion and Training Path	119
Appendix C. Quotes	121
Other books by Toni Crowe, The Writer	124
About the Author	127

Chapter 1
The Corporate World

"The road to success and the road to failure are almost exactly the same."
—Colin R. Davis

"This is a tough place for a woman. I've been put down, pushed aside, knocked out. Truth is I have had to fight my whole life because of who I am, who I love, and where I started. But I didn't let anything get in my way."

These words, spoken by Sharice Davis during her 2018 campaign for Congress, resonated with me immediately. She spoke of her time in the political world, but she might as well have been speaking of my time in corporate America.

I have been working continuously since I was twelve years old. In that time, I have been a play leader, sales clerk, receptionist, medical assistant, laboratory assistant, engineer, senior engineer, program manager, technical manager, manufacturing manager, manufacturing engineering manager, production manager, Director, Site Leader, and Vice President. I have also been President and CEO of my own company. Twice.

Every time I got too comfortable in my career, it bit me. It bit me hard. It took me years to figure out that if I didn't take charge of my career, no one would. It took even longer for me to recognize and act like I was not for sale to the highest bidder. When I worked for a company, I did my best to make them successful, but they had not purchased me. I was allowing them to lease my time, skills, and expertise.

During business hours. I kept my decency, my conscience, and my dignity. This caused me trouble whenever I ran up against "corporate prostitutes." What, you ask, is a corporate prostitute? It is a person who has sold their soul to a company and will do whatever they are told. Anything that is required to meet a company's wants, needs, and goals is acceptable to this person.

I have documented the incidents from my career where there is something to be learned. These are not the most salacious stories, but they are practical stories that can help someone else succeed. These are the universal lessons I wish someone had taught me at earlier. I was successful in my career despite stumbles and bad experiences, and I want to educate and inform whomever I can. No one will need to start from zero once they have read *this book*.

What follows is a series of short stories about the bad bosses in my career. I have deliberately obscured the various companies I worked for, and the stories are not in chronological order. There is no advantage or disadvantage in revealing the companies' identities since these types of incidents occur in all companies. The names have been changed to protect the guilty.

The reason I became a vice president is twofold. While I was working as a senior engineer, I was placed on a team of Ph.D. scientists to facilitate their work on sophisticated equipment. They struggled to work together, and when I arrived, I became both their technician and their workflow facilitator. In other words, I became their boss. Work that had been stalled was completed on time with excellent quality, meeting all of the technical requirements. When I received a bonus equal to 10% of my salary, my husband took me out to dinner.

In our two-engineer home, we usually lived by the unwritten rule that we did not interfere with each other's careers. That night, he gave me a diamond bracelet and some good advice.

Sitting across from me, my husband looked me in the eye and said, "You deserved more than a 10% bonus." He continued, "The team did not work together well until you were added as the 'work facilitator.' Your ability to lead the team made the difference. You should be making your boss's salary."

My mouth gaped open. "What?"

He leaned forward. "Toni, you need to concentrate on becoming a manager."

I stared. "I'm a good engineer—"

"You are a better leader," he interrupted.

It was his input—and that diamond bracelet—that convinced me to apply for a management position.

Many people believe that being the boss is easy. It is not. There are numerous activities that are hidden from the everyday employee that would shock them.

I was working for a toxic boss on a large, important project. The project involved castings, which are made by pouring liquid metal into a sand mold. Manufacturing parts with precision dimensions using this process is something of a magic trick. To add to the challenge, we didn't have molds for this project.

Normally, from start to finish, a casting takes about thirty weeks. We had to make the part samples ourselves, check them, send them to a supplier for machining, check them again, and then send them to a supplier for painting.

We developed a plan for the parts to travel from one supplier to the next, cutting us out as the middleman and bringing the lead time down from thirty weeks twenty-five. On this project, those five weeks could make a huge difference to the production team, which wanted to get the sample parts back in-house as fast as they could to build up first the production prototype and the units themselves.

Both the production team and the parts procurement team reported directly to me. Despite enormous effort on my part and theirs, the parts did not come in at twenty-five weeks. They came in at twenty-six weeks.

They were one week late.

The day the parts were due but did not show up, my boss

stormed into my office. His face was red, he was breathing hard, and his hands were clenched into tight fists. He walked straight toward me, and for a moment, I thought he might punch me.

He climbed up on my desk and started kicking. He kicked my phone off the desk, then my paper clips, then my calendar.

I didn't get out of my seat. I just rolled my chair back against the wall while he was up on my desk kicking things around, hoping I didn't get hit by anything. I was stunned into silence. He was not a skinny man. How upset was he to climb on my desk?

When he had finally kicked everything off, he stared at me. "What was the timeline for this project?"

I told him, "The schedule was thirty weeks."

He didn't like that answer. "What did you tell me you and your team could do?"

"I told you we could get it down to twenty-five weeks."

"Did you get it down to twenty-five weeks?"

"No," I told him, "I did not. I got it down to twenty-six weeks. I apologize for missing the plan by a week and only being four weeks ahead of the original schedule."

This appeared to calm him down a bit. He climbed off my desk.

"Engineering is now behind twelve weeks, and you have only made up nine. I want you to see what you can do to make up the last three weeks we need to be on schedule for this project."

I stood up and pretended that my desk items were not scattered about on the floor.

"Sure. I'll make that happen."

My ability to "make that happen" was one of the reasons I did so well in my career. My second ability to stay calm and take the heat was the second. If you work in manufacturing, operations, or supply chains, there are multiple problems you must solve every day. When you are responsible for all of the parts that are needed to produce revenue products, 99.9% is not good enough. If the plant needs one million parts and you and your team provide 999,999, you have failed.

Manufacturing and Operations are tough gigs. Sometimes, no matter what you achieve, it is never enough.

In thirty-five years, I have changed positions numerous times. Twice, I was fired. One of those times I knew it was coming, but the other time I did not. In both jobs, I had bosses who I believed were my "friends." I had strong relationships with them, and I believed that they would protect me from the other wolves in the organization. I was wrong.

I had grown too comfortable. Corporate America is its own world. Managers, Directors, Vice Presidents, Presidents—none of these people take a job to make friends, because they cannot be friends with their employees. They would be accused of favoritism and could face censure or worst. The higher up the chain you go, the lonelier it is, and the more relevant this quote by Harry Truman becomes: "You want a friend in Washington? Get a dog." Friendship is not a luxury you can afford at work if you desire to be the leader. As the CEO of my own company, I can assure you that being the CEO is the loneliest job in the world. Bullets and bosses don't have friends.

There are three ways to use this book.

The first way is to use it alone. You can sit in your armchair, reading and contemplating my horrific experiences while you compare them to your own.

The second is to read it with a trusted person or peer, then work together to identify the places where these scenarios could potentially occur in your organization.

The third is to form a small weekly discussion group of four to six people and discuss a chapter each week, reviewing the situations and discussing other ways that they could have been handled. Perform the exercises at the end of each chapter together and share your results.

This book works best when shared and discussed. If you can find a peer or colleague of similar intent, engage them. Discussing the stories one-on-one will lead to productive brainstorming about how to avoid these glitches in your company. Often, one person will see what another does not. There is seldom an opportunity to examine your work critically and rationally. This book will help you see clearly.

However, you choose to use this book; it will put you a step ahead of the common problems that bad bosses in corporate America perpetuate. It will give you insight into the actions of your managers and leaders. You will be ahead of the pack. Once you can anticipate your leader's oncoming actions, your career should take off quickly in the right direction.

Good luck, and much success! Now, get your team together and let's get to work.

Chapter 2
Fit in to Get in

"To succeed in life you need two things: ignorance and confidence."
—Mark Twain

The Story

It is critical that anyone who wants to be successful understands what it means to fit in, especially if they are ambitious and want to climb the corporate ladder. It becomes more important if the person is different than the majority in any way—younger, browner, smarter, disabled, or even taller. Not fitting in can significantly decrease your chances of being successful in any organization.

I was working as a production supervisor at a well-known aerospace company in California. The day after Rodney King had been brutally beaten by police, I was headed to a conference room to give a presentation. I was pushing a TV cart down the hall, fully equipped with the audiovisual equipment I needed—a large tube television, VCR, microphone, slide presenter, and numerous pens and pencils. All day, scenes of the previous night's events had run on television. The Rodney King verdict caused much confusion, rioting, and violence. People were breaking into stores, looting whatever they could.

As I rounded a corner, one of my colleagues saw me pushing the cart. He looked at me, startled, and backed away. I had no idea what was wrong, but he left, and I continued on. Within minutes, a security person came around the corner to ask me where I was going with the television set. Then it hit me. They believed I was in the process of looting my own company

I stood there, shocked, and I asked him to call my boss. When my boss arrived, he did not act as I had expected. He asked me to step into the conference room, where he proceeded to lecture me. I was livid. Why would I jeopardize my entire career to steal a ten-year-old TV? Why did he believe that I was stealing it? It must have occurred to him in the middle of the conversation that he might be racist and that I was not attempting to steal the television. After he apologized profusely and made the security guard apologize, they both walked away, red-faced. I was pleased that I had not lost my cool and escalated the situation. My four-month past experience of living in a house with three whores had taught me to control myself no matter what I was accused of.

Over time, I figured out why they had reacted this way to me. I did not participate in any of the sponsored company activities. My home was not far away, but traffic anywhere in the city was terrible. I spent considerable time commuting. I was not on the bowling team, I didn't play baseball, I didn't go to the beach parties, and I seldom went to anyone's house or invited them to mine. I did not attend the after-work celebrations. I had not bothered to fit in. One reason was that I was younger than everyone else. But because I had not taken the time to truly introduce myself to the company, all they saw was a young, ambitious, black woman working hard every day. They did not know my values.

I made it my business to change that. I sat in a row of offices with three other managers of my rank. I began to behave as if their success was important to me. I would stop by their desks to bring them coffee, and I would attend their meetings and support them in their goals. I talked to them about what they wanted to achieve and about what I wanted to achieve. We formed alliances with each other. Between the four of us, we controlled 75% of the resources in the plant. We became a very powerful coalition that made decisions as a team.

The Lesson

The lesson I learned—and one you should follow—is that it is always important that you fit in. You must fit in to get it. People who know and trust you will support you. People who don't know and trust you won't. It is your responsibility to drive the perceptions that people have of you. You must be in control of your career.

Many people believe that the Human Resources Department is responsible for making sure employees are happy and successful, but it is are not. The Human Resources Department exists to protect the human resources of the company. Their job is to keep those human resources productive and safe. You must not depend on anyone other than yourself to shape your reputation at your company. That is your responsibility.

Exercise: Chapter 2

If I asked you today what your reputation was in your organization, could you tell me? Have you taken the time and made an effort to shape how people see you? The perceptions of others, especially those with the power to change your position or your salary, are important.

Get a notebook that you can use to track your exercises throughout this book. You will use this notebook to record observations and answers to exercises every chapter.

As a thank you for purchasing my book, accept the workbook for free. Also available at Amazon.com
http://www.tonicrowewriter.com/bb-workbook-dl-page/

I'd like you to take a moment to write down how you believe you are seen. Then, meet with a colleague and offer to exchange information. You will provide your colleague with an honest perception of what you see, and your colleague will provide you with the same thing.

This exercise will accomplish two things. For one, you will be forced to think of your place in the organization in ways you can explain to others. More importantly, if you take your colleague to lunch off-site for this discussion, it could be the start of a collaboration between the two of you. You should start to build alliances with people who will eventually trust you. Take this action immediately.

No matter where you work, you must fit in to get in. The perception that company employees have of you is as strong as the reality of your personality. If you are ambitious and want to be promoted, then you must be one of the team. Being part of a team invokes trust and acceptance, which is critical to working successfully with the same people day after day.

In the next chapter, we will discuss how important it is to protect your team and stand up for yourself to get ahead. The concept of the team leader protecting the team is ingrained in the corporate culture of America. Good team leaders do not allow their teammates to be abused in any way. They push back, and they empower their members to break the rules to find better solutions.

So, what is push back? To push back is to actively disagree with the direction a conversation is headed in. Pushback can be weak or strong. Strong pushback is normally required when defending your team. When do you need to push back on your boss regarding the people who work for you? Let's examine an incident that required me to resist my boss.

Chapter 3
Protect Your Team

"Don't be distracted by criticism. Remember—the only taste of success some people have is when they take a bite out of you."
—Zig Ziglar

The Story

I was working as a production manager for a Fortune 100 aerospace company. We had taken on a contract that we did not have the ability to deliver in the time allocated. The contract should have taken eighteen months. The allocated timeframe was only seven months.

For the last ten weeks of the project, every single person who worked for me was in-house working twelve hours a day, seven days a week—from the production supervisors to the manufacturing engineers to the facilities employees. We weren't taking our regular lunches. Sometimes I would bring in fast-food, like tacos, and put it in the conference room for people to quickly eat before going back to work. There were other days when everybody would bring a dish, and we would eat from the buffet for most of the day. After working very hard, we were done a full day ahead of schedule. The project shipped, and the company made ridiculous amounts of money.

The next week, I took the entire team—both salaried people and the hourly production team—out to lunch at a Mexican restaurant. We left at 11:30 and didn't return until 2:30, taking an extra-long paid lunch. During lunch, I held a short business discussion about our accomplishments.

When I returned to my office, my boss was waiting for me.

"Can you follow me please?" he asked.

"Sure."

I walked to his office and sat down. He told me that someone had complained that I had taken the entire production team out for a three-hour lunch.

Before I answered, I centered myself. I was angry—*not* a good emotion for critical thinking. I told him in a calm voice that yes, I had absolutely taken the entire production team out for a three-hour lunch. We were celebrating our success in completing a contract in one-third of the standard production time.

That did not satisfy him. He proceeded to lecture me about how it looked for me to take the whole team out for three hours. He explained how embarrassing it was for him that his whole team was gone and he didn't know.

He was right—I should have told him that we were taking a long lunch that day. I apologized for not telling him in advance, but I was angry that he had not defended our team and me knowing the kind of hours we had worked for weeks. I pushed back. "Whoever complained to you," I said, "is welcome to meet me in the lot tomorrow morning at 6:00 AM when I come in, and they're welcome to stay with me until I leave that evening at 6:00 PM. Tell them I'll meet them outside. They can work with me all day. We were working for twelve weeks. After we work together that way for six or seven days it a row, I'll be willing to come and apologize to them for taking the entire team out for a long lunch."

I was usually agreeable, but that day, I was not. My boss stared at me in shock. After a minute, he told me I was dismissed.

No one ever came to take me up on my offer.

The Lesson

The lesson learned is that when someone runs into your office to talk to you about your team, you shouldn't listen only to that person.

Take a moment before you concur and say, "Ah, there's an issue. Let me find out what else is going on, and then I'll see what I can do."

There are *always* two sides to the story. Go find out your team's side. Avoid snap decisions based on one side of the story. There are hidden agendas everywhere in corporate life.

The second thing I learned is that you can demotivate people by not appreciating them. My boss demotivated me by making me feel unappreciated. Don't chastise your team before you do your research and understand exactly what's going on.

Exercise: Chapter 3

Notice that when my boss surprised me, I did not explode. Instead, I centered myself.

Here is an exercise for you to practice. Think of something that makes you angry. Allow yourself to become angry. Now shut it down.

Close the door on the anger. Put it away. You must be able to grab anger at work and put it away immediately. How do I put anger away? Personally, I take five deep breaths, count to ten, then take five more. This works because I have practiced it hundreds of times. You must do the same.

Our next discussion will be about how doing the right thing may put your career at risk. There are times when the right thing is obvious, but no one wants to risk upsetting the apple cart. Sometimes, the apples need to hit the ground.

Chapter 4
Working for a Toxic Boss

"Bosses shape how people spend their days and whether they experience joy or despair, perform well or badly or are healthy or sick. Unfortunately, there are hoards of mediocre and downright rotten bosses out there, and big gaps between the best and the worst. "
—Robert L. Sutton, *Good Boss, Bad Boss: How to Be the Best… and Learn from the Worst*

The Story

I was a purchasing manager and working for another toxic boss—a corporate prostitute. I oversaw the team that procured all the parts and supplies the factory needed. I was in charge of both the direct and indirect spending, totaling about $44 million for the factory. We were a small division.

My boss, who I'll call Abraham, was toxic the entire time he worked for the company. The problem with working for such a boss is that he affects everything around him. Toxicity spreads like wildfire, as these three incidents vividly show.

Abraham had no idea how to treat people, and it was causing us to lose the experts we needed. One of these instances happened at a monthly staff meeting, which everyone in the department attended. We were introducing the new casting engineer. Casting engineers are very hard to find because there are so many different types of castings, requiring them to have a range of complicated technical knowledge and skills. It took us a year or two to fill the position. This casting engineer was doing a fantastic job. We had gone from having significant problems with our castings to having only small problems.

We were at our staff meeting. The casting engineer worked directly for Abraham since he was a technical specialist. He was sitting in his seat when Abraham walked over, balled up a piece of paper in his hand, and threw it at him. He caught the piece of paper.

Abraham said, "That's your expense report. You're missing a receipt for the gas used on your supplier visit."

The engineer looked at him and said, "Okay, I'll get it."

Abraham balled up another piece of paper and threw it at him. He said, "These are the receipts that you did give me."

He continued to stand there and, one at a time, ball up pieces of paper that the casting engineer had turned in with his expense report and throw them at him.

The rest of us just sat there in shock. By the end of five minutes, the engineer was surrounded by balled up pieces of paper that were formerly his expense report. It was clear that

Abraham was enjoying his discomfort.

Once he had thrown all of the paper, Abraham simply moved on to the next subject. The casting engineer sat in his seat, surrounded by balls of paper. I never saw him pick them up. I don't even know if he did, because as soon as the meeting was over, I stood up and beat it out of there.

Within two weeks, the casting engineer was gone. It probably took him a week to get a job somewhere else. He gave one week's notice and left the company. Once he left, we advertised for another casting engineer, but we never found one. The plethora of problems we had been having with castings slowly worked their way back into our systems. Six months after he left, I heard someone say, "I sure wish we had kept that casting engineer." I did too.

At a different point during my time with this company, we had a transsexual person in our department—a man who was transitioning into a woman. In the midst of this change, he wanted to stop using the men's restroom and start using the women's restroom. We had no policy to address this situation, so Abraham wrote one. The policy was delivered to HR. HR sent him home for two days. I had no idea what that policy said, and I never asked.

HR asked me to write the policy since the gentleman had spoken with me and provided some documents. I wrote one, and when Abraham returned to work and read it, he became furious that he had not been allowed to rewrite the policy. He said mine was too liberal. He went to HR, and once again, HR sent him home for a couple of days.

I can't imagine what his policy said.

There is one more incident involving Abraham that I would like to relate, the most stunning of them all.

It was late in the day. We had another of those crazy staff meetings. This time, Abraham had chosen one of our good associates—an independent, quiet person, not exceptionally special—as his target. He was one of those people who you knew would complete a project well, meeting all your expectations. Just a solid, good, working person.

Abraham made him cry. We're not talking silent tears rolling down his cheeks either—we're talking loud, audible sobbing. Abraham criticized him viciously because he had been assigned to pull in some special parts at reduced cost and he had been unable to do so.

We sat there while Abraham compared current costs to desired costs to actual costs, part by part for every single piece the gentleman controlled. Abraham relished every place where the reductions were not met. By the end of the meeting, the gentleman was sobbing.

The only person who interrupted Abraham during this tirade was me. I pointed out that some of these parts had never met the desired costs in the history of my employment at the company. If we wanted to meet these cost targets, I suggested, perhaps we needed to put together a focused cost reduction team. I knew I would pay for those interruptions later, but by then I didn't care. I wasn't going to sit idle and let his abuse continue with no opposition.

When I arrived at work the next day, the shamed employee was waiting for me outside of my office. I went in and sat down.

He followed me, and when I turned toward him, he said, "I just wanted to let you know that I appreciate you standing up for me. And I appreciate you trying to take care of me."

Okay, I thought. *I guess he's going to quit.* I dreaded what he would say next. He was a good worker who had an expert knowledge of parts that other people did not. I could not afford to lose him.

But that's not what he told me. In a deadly calm voice, he said, "I'm going to kill Abraham."

In normal circumstances, I suppose such a declaration would have elected a response of shock and horror. Such a response would have accomplished nothing and in fact would have made things worst, so I kept it together. This was now a high stakes situation.

"If you kill Abraham... Well, there's a problem with that."

He said, "What problem?"

I paused. "Let's go to another area to talk about this."

We left my office and went to one of the small lobby offices in the front. I was more comfortable here since these were all glass and security was always in the lobby. We sat down.

"I'm going to kill him when I finish talking to you," he said. "I am fed up with the way he treats other people and me."

"You know that if you kill him, I'm going to have to fire you."

I couldn't believe I was talking to someone about murder. The consequences would be so much greater than me firing him, but it was all I could think to say. Besides that, he seemed to believe that he could kill one of the PresidentsVice Presidents and still keep his job. I couldn't argue with him about the way he felt. I was there and saw that horrific treatment. But you just don't murder people at work. Murdering is against the law.

"If you kill somebody on company property, I am going to fire you." I paused. "Go home. Take a paid day off. You need to get out of here."

When he came back the next day, he had regained his senses. "Just because he's a jerk doesn't mean I have to act like a jerk too," he told me. They were words of wisdom from a person who had been so upset.

The next week, he came back and thanked me for knowing what to say to stop him in his tracks. He believed that no logical argument would have had any effect on his chosen course of action. I didn't use arguments. I just said, "If you kill him, I will fire you, and then you won't have a job." That ended up being the key.

So, I've told you about three horrific incidents caused by one man caused during the three months I worked for him. What was the straw that finally broke my back, you ask? It took one staff meeting where he drew down on everyone and told us all how lazy and stupid we were to know I needed a different position.

The Lesson

When you work for a toxic person, you must take care not to infuriate them while trying to do your job. Most people are not as toxic as Abraham was. Some people just have a touch of it. You need to keep that poisonous mix from being poured on you while your head is down working hard. The lesson learned was that a toxic boss affects every employee. People who are working for this person do not want to work for him, and they are considered damaged goods if they work for him too long. It took me until the second staff meeting to speak up, and that was not like me. The toxicity in the first meeting affected me, and I froze. I would not have lasted long in that position.

Once again, serendipity was on my side. A production manager job opened unexpectedly. I was not laterally transferred but promoted to the production floor by the President. He was the only person who could overrule Abraham. The president decided to move me because there was no way the production floor could operate without supervision. Abraham would do my job and run the purchasing department.

I took that new assignment so fast. The atmosphere, the very air you breathe, turns poisonous working for a toxic boss.

Exercise: Chapter 4

Imagine how you would handle a toxic boss. What are five steps that you would take to ensure that your career survived? Record in your workbook.

Next chapter, we will examine how to deal with an ongoing situation where no action has been taken but needs to be. There are times when leaders must step up to the plate. The trick is knowing when to spend that capital. No one can fight every battle and win. Fighting on too many fronts is a time-honored technique for losing.

Chapter 5
Dick in His Hand

"Unless someone like you cares a whole awful lot,
it's not going to get better. It's not."
—Dr. Seuss

The Story

I was working as a Director. My boss, one of the PresidentsVice Presidents, was a "good old boy" of the Fortune 50 company.

One day, I was walking past a conference room when I noticed a young woman sitting in the dark. She was a cleaning lady, and she had her head down on the table, sobbing.

I went in to find out what was wrong. When I spoke to her, she told me that she had had enough. She had reported a problem several times, but no one had done anything about it.

"Well, tell me," I offered. "I'm new in the building."

She told me that one of the PresidentsVice Presidents—not my boss—had waited for her to come to clean his office.

When she came in, he had his pants unzipped and his dick in his hand. The entire time that she was in there cleaning, he was rubbing himself and leering at her.

I was stunned.

I asked, "Are you certain he has his dick in his hand, and he's doing that? And you reported this?"

She nodded. "I reported it to my supervisor, and to some of the other managers here. I even reported it to your HR, but no one can stop him because he only does it when I'm alone with him."

I said, "Well, did they ever go with you?"

She nodded her head. "Yes." They had walked around with her, but they'd made a lot of noise as they approached his office. When they went into his office, he was sitting at the desk, working. The very next time she came by herself, he was sitting there with his dick in his hand.

I was disgusted. "Well, we can do something about this," I told her. "Tomorrow, before you go in there, come and get me."

The next day, she came and got me. I stood out of sight while she was cleaning. When we got to his office, I asked her to stand outside. I pushed the cleaning cart into the office. Sure enough, when I walked in, he was pushed back from his desk with his legs spread wide, his pants unzipped, and his dick in his hand. When he saw me, he jumped up and quickly stuffed his dick back in his pants and zipped them up. But it was too late. I had seen it all.

He laughed. "They already know." I took that to mean he thought I was powerless.

The next morning I approached my boss, his equal, and said, "I went into his office. He had his dick in his hand, stroking it when I walked into the room."

My boss stared at me. "What?"

I said it again. "I walked into his office. He had his dick in his hand, stroking it when I walked into the room."

My boss was standing very still, silent.

I felt my temper rise. "You didn't hear me. I need some kind of reaction right now. I just told you that I just walked into a room in this big, respectable company with incredibly deep pockets, and one of the Vice Presidents had his dick in his hand and was stroking it."

My boss looked at me, and I stared back. After a moment, his attitude changed. He became excited, enraged, and angry that such a thing had happened to me.

We talked for a while before I asked, "What will be done about this?"

The next thing I knew, I was in an office behind a closed door with a group of people trying to tell me that I had not seen a dick. This team didn't know my history of living with prostitutes. I'm not uncomfortable talking about dicks. Still, they asked what should have been embarrassing questions: "What color was the dick?" "Was it hard or soft?" "How was he stroking it?"

I was forced to talk about this guy with his dick in his hand at work. I answered every question clearly and concisely. We never mentioned the cleaning lady or how long this horrific behavior had been going on for.

"I know what a dick looks like. I've been married for 20

years. He had his dick in his hand. He was stroking it, and he was staring at me." I continued, furious. "Do you guys want me to show you *how* he had his dick in his hand? If you want me to demonstrate for you, I can try. I don't know what you want me to do, but I'm not going to be at work with a man who is going to randomly have his dick in his hand. I don't know if he's going to have his dick in his hand the next time I walk into his office. Or if he has his dick in his hand right next to me at a meeting. What if he's walking around with his dick in his hand right now, showing it to everybody? We must do something about this."

I would not budge. Later that day, the company announced that he was unexpectedly retiring.

I had to be strong. I could not allow them to intimidate me about something so ridiculous. You can't just display your genitalia at work. It was not right that he had been terrorizing one of the lowest-level employees in the building. He was harassing a person with no power. To make matters worse, it was ridiculous that people thought the cleaning lady was making up a story about the Vice President holding his dick. If I hadn't been the person in the room, they would have intimidated whoever else reported him into believing their eyes were lying.

In the Marx Brothers' film *Duck Soup*, Chico asks a woman, "Who are you going to believe, me or your eyes?" For a moment there, I felt like I was in the movie.

The Lesson

I ran away with a pimp when I was eighteen, and ever since then, I easily recognize intimidation tactics. You can't let them trap you. You can't let anyone beat you down. You must stand up to intimidation. When you work for a company as a manager, you are in a leadership role. When you are being paid to be a leader, you should do anything for your company, as long as it isn't illegal or immoral. It is illegal *and* immoral for a man to have his dick in his hand, showing it to a powerless woman.

You can work for a company and retain your values. There was no reason not to dismiss that person. He put the company in danger of multiple criminal charges while recklessly seeking personal pleasure. I refuse to be party to illegal or criminal actions because I'm not going to jail for anyone.

The rule for handling illegal and immoral acts in a company is simple when you are in a leadership position: Once you know about it, you must do something. You must behave in a legal and moral fashion.

Exercise: Chapter 5

In your notebook, write down what you would do when confronted with an illegal or immoral situation at your workplace. How would you behave? Record the things you would consider before deciding whether or not to take action. Understanding yourself will be key when such a decision is forced upon you. Having already considered what you might do will provide you with an edge when if you are involved in an incident.

The situation involving Jerry Sandusky at Penn State is an example of people not acting when they should have. Numerous individuals knew or suspected that there was abuse, but none of them acted. As a result, many young lives were impacted that should not have been. No one was willing to speak truth to power.

Next up, we are going to review how becoming the best in your chosen field is nothing but goodness for your career. It is a pleasure to be very good at what you do and be rewarded and appreciated for your skill and talent.

Chapter 6
Be an Expert

"To be a champion, I think you have to see the big picture. It's not about winning and losing; it's about the everyday hard work and about thriving on a challenge. It's about embracing the pain that you'll experience at the end of a race and not being afraid. I think people think too hard and get afraid of a certain challenge."

—Summer Sanders

The Story

I was working as an associate engineer for a very large, very reputable aerospace company when they assigned me to work for a senior man named Mr. Johnson. He had a reputation as a hard-drinking, loud laughing, prank-playing, redheaded womanizer. He must have been about eighty years old. He sat in an air-conditioned office built especially for him in the technical basement of the plant, far away from everyone else. He was the only living expert on equipment that was key to the company's success. My desk was placed right next to his office.

Since he was older, the company wanted to transfer his knowledge to someone else. Johnson was very resistant to the company's efforts. They tried getting people who were his equals, as well as other very technical people, to work with him. One of the problems they kept running into was that he did not have an engineering degree and didn't like people who did.

The company tried assigning recent college graduates to him, but those people didn't work out either. Within a month of working for him, young graduates would request a transfer out of the department, just like the older people who had worked for him before them. The company even tried to partner him with people from another large aerospace company, but he would not cooperate with them either. Within thirty days, they would request a transfer away from him.

Even without an engineering day, this man remains the best technical engineer I have ever met. He was a natural mechanical wizard. I've only ever met one engineer who I believe matched him. I married that guy.

Johnson had been involved with the beginnings of this equipment. He had helped design it and knew how to repair and run the equipment. Once, when Johnson was on vacation, the equipment broke down. No one knew what to do. By the time he returned, the company had lost a tremendous amount of money.

When they assigned me to Johnson, I didn't realize that

he was a problem. I didn't know any better. It was the most money I had ever made in my lifetime, and I wasn't going anywhere. I had a husband and two children to take care of. At that time, it never occurred to me that I could transfer.

Johnson began testing me to see if he could get me to leave the organization. He would send me off to perform ridiculous technical experiments on the equipment. I would run those experiments exactly how he asked me to. I would record the data fastidiously and compile it in a report. One day, I arrived at work to find one of my reports sitting on my desk. The darn thing was twenty pages long. It had taken me about four, maybe five, weeks to run the experiments, collect and analyze the data, and write the report. Mr. Johnson had marked through *every single line* on that report and told me to rewrite it.

I wrote the report again. After I gave it to him, he marked it up again, and I wrote a third report.

This time, he was finally satisfied. "Now, that's the level of report I want," he said. "I want this level of excellence and nothing less."

He would call random late-night meetings with random late-night assignments. He was "jerking my chain," choking me with assignments to see if I would last. Finally, after I had worked for him for ninety days, he took me out for a nice lunch. He said that I was too stupid to quit or transfer. Since I was determined to stay with him, he would teach me what he knew. I was pleasantly surprised.

In the next eight months, I got two promotions as a result of my work with Mr. Johnson. He showed me exactly what it took to diagnose, understand, rework, and calibrate the equipment that no one else understood. Once I knew how the equipment worked, I became invaluable to the company.

It turned out that once you got to know Mr. Johnson and he accepted you, the real work began. His efforts to get rid of me were nothing like his efforts to teach me. The teaching was much worst. It was like drinking from a fire hose.

Mr. Johnson did not retire while I was at that company. If he had retired, things would have been fantastic for me. As it was, the moment I understood how the equipment worked, he authorized me to train others. His legacy was preserved.

The Lesson

There are three lessons to take away from this story. The first is that you can't judge a book by its cover. We all know this to be true. Mr. Johnson was a bent-over, red-headed, feisty, little old man who was very good at what he did.

The second lesson is that perseverance counts. I was persistent, and I dealt with everything that he threw at me. I focused on the work. The report is an excellent example of this, as the final product was excellent. One of the reasons I was promoted was that, because of Johnson's demanding nature, I grew from being technically average to technically excellent.

Finally, the third lesson is that if you can land a position working for someone smarter than you, do so. Working for an expert in your industry can and will make a huge difference to your success.

Exercise: Chapter 6

Identify at least five jobs in your current company that are attractive to you. One must be two levels above your current position. Research the qualifications and job requirements for each of these. Now, list the skills and job requirements for your current position.

How many of your current qualifications and requirements are prerequisites for each of the positions you desire? If there is less than a 60% match, then you will be prevented from obtaining that position.

Take a moment and compare the disconnects. Determine if you can prevail over the gap between where you are and where you want to be. You may need training to get there, or it may be a matter of assignments. Whatever the disconnect, you must close that gap if you want to be a competitive applicant for a position.

In our next chapter, we explore the unhealthy effect that an environment perceived as unfair has on team dynamic and productivity.

Chapter 7
Know the Unwritten Rules

"Leaders must exemplify integrity and earn the trust of their teams through their everyday actions. When you do this, you set high standards for everyone in the company. And when you do so with positive energy and enthusiasm for shared goals and purpose, you can deeply connect with customers."
—Marilyn Henson

The Story

I was working for a midsize sensor and motor drive company. During my time as a Director, I ran into something that threw me for a loop. Even to this day, I don't fully understand it. At the company, it was common practice to hire family and friends. There were family groups everywhere—husbands, wives, children, cousins, daughters, uncles. As long as a person could perform the job requirements, it was fine with HR.

The issues came when hired friends could not perform

the job. Those situations caused chaos. Anyone incompetent was booted out soon after they arrived. Gossipers and troublemakers did not last long either.

Directors had full authority to hire whomever they wanted. The company seldom disapproved of anyone. This was a freedom that I loved. I started hiring different types of people. I hired a lot of women. I attracted people from out of state. And I hired minorities.

After working there for two years, the HR Director approached me in my office. She challenged me, saying that I had a discernible pattern of hiring people who were like me.

I thought for a minute, then said, "You know what? You are right. I am hiring people who are like me."

For a moment, she thought she had me. She leaned back and smiled.

"However," I continued, "if we're going to use that as a criterion for hiring, we need a much bigger meeting than just you and me. Because the men—white men—who dominate this company are hiring white men. So, we have white men hiring white men. Some of them have hired no one *but* white men as long as I have been here."

Silence descended on my small office. She took my unspoken point—that if you're going to come into my office and talk to me about what I'm doing, I'm going to call you on it, and we are going to talk about everyone.

Before she left my office, she concurred that there was not an issue and that I could keep doing whatever I was doing.

The Lesson

The moral of this story is to stand your ground if you are right. If you are following an unwritten policy, don't argue with them. Agree. As you agree, reach out and pull in other interesting examples to support your case. When you've done this, they must apply whatever they do to you to everyone.

That's the lesson learned here. Know the rules. Follow the rules. Also, know the unwritten rules, and follow the unwritten rules, but to be ready to defend yourself if you need to.

Exercise: Chapter 7

Identify the unwritten rules in your company. List at least three in your workbook. What would you do if accused of breaking these unspoken rules?

In the next chapter, we are going to discuss how those knives get slipped into your back, sometimes by those that you have worked with and trusted for long periods of time. It is hard to remember that the people you see five days a week, 8 hours a day are not your family or your friends but your work colleagues

Chapter 8
If You Are Leaving, Leave

"The secret to success is to know something nobody else knows."
Aristotle Onassis

The Story

I was the site leader in charge of two divisions at a Fortune 50 aerospace company. My boss, a vice president, was from another country. I'd been with the business for four years, and it was doing very well. We were meeting all our goals: profit and loss, Earnings Before Interest and Taxes (EBIT), quality. Our balance sheet financials were on point. We had improved our quality by more than 40%. We were hiring great new people. The team was shaping up.

I met a corporate VP of another division of my company one of our corporate training events. The VP was in charge of lean and productivity for the entire company. They worked directly for the CEO of the organization, which meant they outranked even my boss. They invited me to interview for an opening that would have me report to someone directly under the CEO, moving me up the ladder a level.

I interviewed well and won the position. I would need to move my family, but the promotion would include an increase in status and pay.

Nevertheless, when I put in for the position, my boss flew to my location. He came into my office, sat down, and talked to me for more than three hours. We went out to lunch. He built an entire scenario to show where I could go in his organization and why the other organization was not good for me. He had charts and graphs to show me how I was part of his personal "think tank." He really needed me. If I continued to do as well as I was doing, the pathway he offered was quicker and better. He offered to raise my salary to the amount I had been offered to take the promotion if I would stay in my position.

It seemed like a good deal. The positions he offered me were better than the position I would have been taking. His offer would allow me to oversee another factory in the division I had, and that seemed significant. I turned down the position that I was offered by the other vice president. I told them I had changed my mind, and that I was going to remain in my current position. It took them about a month to fill the job.

Then, two months later, I was called in by the same boss who had all but promised me future promotions. He put me on a performance improvement plan. What, you ask, is a performance improvement plan? It's a plan for people who are doing poorly—a common way to tell an individual,

"Hey, you know what? You are on your way out of the company."

Normally, there's a detailed process with checkpoints that you must go through to place a person on a performance improvement plan. At the lower levels of this company, a person first received a friendly warning. Then they would get a verbal warning. Next, they would get a written warning. Then, and only then, could you put them on a performance improvement plan. If you followed this pathway, there would be no doubt that the person had been informed that they weren't doing well.

However, at the higher levels of the company, none of that documentation was required. All the boss needed to do was say, "You're performing badly." I went from being fantastic to being horrific, but the only thing that had changed was that I had attempted to take a different position. All my metrics had stayed the same. We were still beating our profit and our sales. We still had excellent quality. We were still building great teams. But I had "betrayed" my boss by attempting to leave the organization. As soon as he had the opportunity, he punished me by putting me on a performance improvement plan.

I ended up leaving the position because the performance improvement plan was like dancing on hot coals. No matter what I did, there was always another bullet on that plan when I came in to see him—*not* the way it is supposed to work. The way the plan *should* work is that you are given a defined amount of time to straighten up. These are supposed to be "SMART" goals—Specific, Measurable, Achievable,

Reasonable, and Timed. I didn't have SMART goals. I had dumb goals, all of which were made up. As soon as I dodged one bullet, a new, unique bullet would show up. I swear to God, one of my bullets was that I was not allowed to have meetings at 5:00 p.m. Every manager called late meetings, but somehow, I was no longer allowed to schedule these routine late meetings.

My boss had dissuaded me from taking another position by appearing to be my friend and mentor. He provided advice on how I could achieve success in his organization. It was not true. Bullets and bosses don't have friends.

The Lesson

The moral of this story is that if you tell them you're going to leave, you must leave. It doesn't matter if you are leaving for a transfer, or if you are leaving for another organization in the same company. It doesn't matter if you are leaving the company altogether. You must leave. There is no reversal. One way or another, your boss will punish you for your lack of loyalty. I did not know that at this point in my career. Before this moment, any time I had decided to leave, I left. This was the only time that I ever turned around and stayed. I never repeated that mistake.

made this mistake for you. You have no excuse to repeat it. You cannot unring the bell.

Exercise Chapter 8

In your workbook, capture the following:

before notifying your boss that you are leaving, consider what it would take to cause you to change your mind to stay.

Once you turn the page, we are going to discuss in depth the reason that small public divisions and private companies have plenty of risk and opportunity associated with them. In short, private companies do not publicly report their earning and expenses, so their actual performance is known by few. Small divisions are often run by a clique of long-term managers. Understanding the risks is key to your success.

Chapter 9
Understand Your Environment

"Success is not final, failure is not fatal: it is the courage to continue that counts."
—Winston Churchill

The Story

At one point, I had given up work and moved to be near my sick mom. After she passed away, I decided to return to corporate America. Although I had plenty of experience in manufacturing operations, and increasing profit by improving productivity, I was having trouble finding a position near my mom.

I interviewed for a job working in a small division of a larger company. The division had been taken over by one family. The mother was the president and CEO, the father was the facility manager, and the son was the organization's lawyer. I became the Director of manufacturing, a position that appeared to be perfect for me. I reported to the vice president, who was not a family member.

The company had developed a particular circuit board—a board of electrical circuits that is installed in a larger piece of equipment—that the U.S. government was using. They had signed an Indefinite Delivery, Indefinite Quantity (IDIQ) contract. The U.S. government had only been using four of these products a month when they suddenly increased the quantity to four hundred a month. The small company was failing miserably to meet the high demand. I was hired to bring the company up to speed using productivity techniques. The goal was to be meeting the U.S. government's demands within six months.

The issues, it turned out, were not with the product or the people who worked on the product. The issues were with the family in charge. There were innumerable instances of blatantly unfair treatment resulting from the family's feelings, of which I will share only a few. Facts did not make a dent in their activities.

The company was built to have a four-day work week, ten hours each day. The management team, however, did not work ten-hour days. Our jobs required us to work between twelve and fifteen hours a day, Monday through Thursday.

The President, who did not work on Mondays, insisted on having a weekly management meeting every Friday with all Vice Presidents and Directors. The meetings lasted between four and six hours. Altogether, the management team worked a minimum of fifty hours per week.

The second crazy thing was the fact that no Director had worked there for more than two years. It was a mysterious but universal trend that Directors turned incompetent after one year and eleven months. The truth, of course, was that they were fired to ensure that no one would gather enough power to challenge the family's influence.

The third issue was that, somehow, executive bonuses were never paid, no matter the performance. One year, the team met all the stretch goals except for "orders booked," despite how ridiculous they were. On the 29th of December, the facility was closed when a huge order came in, hitting our "orders booked" goal and triggering a 25% bonus for the management team.

The Directors never received our bonuses for that year. The company officially booked the order in January to avoid paying us the extra 25%.

To top it all off, there was a bad smell around the way they treated people. There was one gentleman working for me who the president did not like. At the company performance "rack and stack," where employees are arranged in order of their perceived values, he dropped the employee ten spaces. When I protested and convinced the other Directors to move him back up five spaces, he came after me for not addressing my own problems. What he considered to be my "problems" were invented at best. At my performance review, he told me I was the best he had ever seen in operations—certainly in the top 1%. Then he told me that my raise had been lowered because I was in the bottom of the top 1%. I gawked. What on earth did that mean?

A year later, this employee left the company. When he

did, he told the president that he felt that his work was put under extra scrutiny by his boss—me. It was true that I double-checked anything he turned in to the president. When my boss, the vice president, called me in to discuss the employee's parting complaints, I reminded him that the president was the one who had examined his work so critically. He denied any such thing and gave me a verbal warning for my actions.

About a month later, the President decided that he disliked a different employee in my organization. I knew that my technique of overanalyzing her work would not prevent issues. This time, I brought the employee into my office and had a frank discussion with her about the perception of her work. I asked her to double and triple check anything that was being turned in to our leaders. I pointed out that making sure her work was perfect was the key to her success. She responded by providing excellent work that could seldom be criticized. This addressed the issue with the president in a much more positive way.

This unfair treatment reached all the way up to their bosses. The vice president of sales had reached one year and eleven months with the company. When he came to work that day, his office key did not work. He went to the facilities building, where he found the president and HR waiting for him. They fired him on the spot and walked him out of the building. Five minutes later a new vice president of sales walked down the stairs. They opened the office door, and he went into the office and sat down.

The Lesson

Small divisions can behave like private companies when corporate is physically and mentally far away. The management team can do whatever they choose with few consequences. When a small number of individuals control the entire division or company, managers, Directors, and PresidentsVice Presidents are required to think of unique ways to be successful. Working for a small division or private company is fine, as long as the position is taken with the knowledge of what could happen.

I eventually left the organization. After working there for one year and ten months, I found another position, knowing I would have been fired shortly.

The Exercise

Small organizations with a few managers holding power are both dangerous and full of opportunity. In your workbook, draw two columns. Write the word "Pro" in one column, and in the other write the word "Con." Take a moment to think about small organizations. List the opportunities available when working for a small company in the "Pro" column. List the risks of working for a small company in the other. As you examine your lists, it will become apparent whether or not you should work for a small organization. Repeat this exercise when you identify a small company you would like to work for using the particular attributes of that company to make your Pro and Con List.

Chapter 10
Golden Boys

> "Nearly all men can stand adversity, but if you want to test a man's character, give him power."
> —Abraham Lincoln

The Story

It is unfortunate, but golden boys—extremely popular and successful men—are usually white men with connections. I once interviewed with a golden boy who was, at the time, a vice president. I was a Director, and within the golden boy's sphere of influence. During the interview, we were discussing the difficulty of finding executive jobs. He said, "I have never had to interview for a job in my life."

To make sure I understood, I asked, "How did you get this job?" He answered that one of his father's friends had called him up and asked if he wanted the job. He insisted that he needed to see the plant before answering. He came in, saw his beautiful office view from a top floor, and accepted the position.

To be clear, a golden boy is a man, competent or incompetent, who is regarded as wonderful no matter what he does at the company. He can make any mistake and still be promoted. You don't want to work for a golden boy, and you don't want a golden boy working for you. You don't want to sit next to a golden boy. You don't want to park next to a golden boy. You don't want to be involved with a golden boy. Golden boys suck all of the air out of the room.

It doesn't matter if the golden boy likes you. He's not good for you. It doesn't matter if the golden boy doesn't like you. He's still not good for you. The glow around this man is so glaring that, no matter what you do, you get sunburned.

This chapter should be shorter. I could have just stopped right after I said, "Golden boys: avoid them at all costs." But I'll give you two examples of golden boys—one who liked me, and how it got me into trouble, and another who hated me, also getting me into trouble.

Let's talk about the one who liked me first. This golden boy was the boss's son. He couldn't work for the boss, but he could work for someone who worked for the boss. So, he worked for me. He was arrogant, charming, attractive, and very smart. He could have worked elsewhere, but he chose to work for his mother's company

I did my work, and much of the time, I did his work. He and I were the production managers, and I was the senior manager. His team fed mine. When I was on the floor, I directed both our teams. He sat in his office reading the paper and drinking a soda or walked around the cafeteria talking to people. Anyone else who did that much reading, talking, and walking would have been called by human resources and spoken to. He was not.

He paid no attention to the rules. Once, we went to a Mexican restaurant for lunch. He drove. When we arrived, he ordered a margarita with lunch. I had an iced tea.

We returned from lunch terribly late. He went to his office and sat down. I walked back to mine, where I found HR waiting for me. They called me in and told me that other employees had seen him drinking the margarita. The human resources person leaned across the desk. "How could you let him drink a margarita, where everyone can see it? We're very disappointed in your behavior."

"What?" I protested. "Disappointed in my behavior? I drank iced tea. I wasn't drinking margaritas."

"If you're going to go out to lunch, you need to make sure that we don't have these problems again."

I thought to myself, *Am I a babysitter? He is going to break or bend the rules no matter what they are. I don't want to go out with him. I don't want to be seen with him.* But of course, there's no way to tell a golden boy no—especially when he's your boss's son.

This next example is of a golden boy who hated me from the moment he walked in. He was arrogant as hell and short with Napoleon Complex. I often wore my heels so that I could be taller than him. In fact, I was already a head taller; with my heels on, I was two heads taller.

He was an expert in his field; I had to give him that. But he was stupid in every other field. He would read a book, then believe that he could do the job of a person with thirty-five years' experience. Sitting on staff with a golden boy was a challenge. He could say something, and the boss's head would nod vigorously. Then you could say that exact same thing, and the boss's head would shake back and forth.

The worst part was that this incompetent, unqualified buffoon had the same vote that I had in our staff meetings even though he worked directly for me. And was my subordinate. It made staff meetings tense and very unhappy. I was frequently called out for trying to discuss people issues. Even when what I wanted to do was clearly the right thing, the golden boy might say, "I don't want to do that." Because there were only eight of us, if a few others agreed with him, then suddenly people jumped to his side because it was fun to see the executives debate. .

This man abused his staff where everyone could hear and see it. They would walk around with their heads down, creating a motivation problem for everyone else. My staff wanted to know why I didn't do anything about it. I went in to talk to HR and the president and quickly realized that was the wrong thing to do. From a moral standpoint, of course, it was right, but not for my career. After I spoke to them about his behaviors, HR talked to the people he was abusing. Those people suddenly wouldn't admit they were being abused.

The next thing I knew, I was being investigated for telling lies about the golden boy. Lies that weren't lies—lies that were true. Ultimately, I was pushed out of the company. Luckily, I was pushed into taking a better position; unluckily the promotion was at a terrible location.

The Lesson

The first lesson here is to stay away from golden boys. Don't mess with them. Will Rogers said that "Diplomacy is the art of saying 'nice doggie' until you can find a rock." This should be your golden boy philosophy. Don't become their enemy *or* their friend. Their glow will not reflect on you; it will burn your career opportunities away. Put on some career sunscreen and walk away. Secondly, don't defend the employees of other leaders without knowing that those employees are willing to defend themselves. If something illegal is going on, you must always step up, no question. However, if the issue is in a soft subject and open to interpretation, make sure those you are defending want to be defended. If they won't speak up for themselves, you will end up looking like a jackass just like I did. I paid a steep price for not taking a moment to talk to those employees before going to HR.

Exercise: Chapter 10

Take a moment to catalog who in your organization is a golden boy. Most organizations have at least one. Now, focus on how you will handle situations with this person. To protect your career, you must always have a plan to deal with these superstars. Write your plan in your career notebook.

In the next chapter, we are going to discuss why it pays to understand your workflow. Knowing where you work comes from and where your work goes is essential. This axiom is true even if the work gets passed between departments in a large corporation.

Chapter 11
Who Is Your Customer?

"Don't live down to expectations. Go out there and do something remarkable."
—Wendy Wasserstein.

The Story

I was straight out of school and had landed a job with a Fortune 50 company. They hired a significant number of new graduates that year because they had recently won a large contract to update existing equipment. Understand that this is nothing like it is on TV, where people graduate from school and suddenly become a fabulously rich engineer working on wonderful new equipment. No. I was working as an associate engineer, which, by the way, is a shit job.

Every day, I updated senior engineers' old designs. This was work that nobody wanted to do, so it was always assigned to the newest engineers. To update old designs, an engineer had to understand how the old designs worked, then understand the update. The engineer who did the original design may or may not still be in your department, so you couldn't always ask questions. Once you understood the original and the update, you had to make a modification to the circuit or mechanical parts to meet the new requirements.

Working with someone else's work made this a challenging task. If the person forgot to draw even a single line, or if they modified something after the drawings were complete, your design would not work. You would have to start all over once you truly understood what the old design did. Plus, you had to go back in time, read the old specifications, then get your new modification tested. It then had to be certified and sometimes needed to be requalified. The whole process could take years.

This was a very frustrating job. The good news was that I was older than the other new graduates. Better yet, my eighteen-year-old self's experience with a pimp made me cool-headed.

Well, more cool-headed than the other associates.

I had five design updates. Four of the five were completed, and I had done a good job; those four were fully approved. The fifth was another story. I could not figure it out. No matter what I did, every time I sent the thing to pre-test, it failed. I'd go back and re-read the old specs. Then I'd go and re-read the new specs. I'd figure out what I could change again, and I'd send the design update back down. It would still fail.

After twelve weeks of pure failure, frustration got the better of me, and I decided to do something highly unusual. I decided to go down to the production floor and observe them testing my design.

When I went downstairs to meet with the production people, I accidentally came during their lunchtime. They were having a party, complete with cake, pizza, and soda. When I walked in, they invited me to join them.

I don't think they recognized that I was an engineer. I came right in and shared their lunch. We talked and had a good time. Then, when lunch was over, one guy asked, "What are you down here for?"

"I'm Crowe," I said. "I came down to see why my design keeps failing."

They all burst out laughing. "Your design is bad. It's never going to work."

"Well, you guys never sent anything back. All you sent me back was a report that said it failed."

"Yes."

"You never gave me any recommendations."

"We aren't asked for recommendations."

"You never said what I could do."

"That's not our job. Our job is to test it and tell you if it passed or failed."

One of the guys took pity on me and said, "Listen, the reason your design will never work is that there's another set of designs you need to consider further down in the system."

I was surprised. "But when I looked at all the documentation associated with this update, it didn't say anything about another system that could affect my design."

They all laughed again. "No, it doesn't say anything about it. You have to figure that out."

I thought to myself, *How can I figure that out if nobody*

even gave me a hint about what to look for? Out loud, I said, "What do you think I should do?"

There was dead silence. I stood there for a moment, looked at them again, and repeated my question. "What do you think I should do?"

"Nobody ever asks us that," one of them said. "No one's ever come down here."

"My design doesn't work. What do you think I should do? I'm asking. I'm asking because I'm late with this design. I can't send the other four up without all five, and I've already wasted so much time trying to figure this out. I would appreciate it if you guys would give me a hand."

In the end, they helped me put my design together. Working with them was fun. I had a dry sense of humor and a talent for making jokes. They didn't see me as an engineer from upstairs, which I believe helped me considerably. When I sent it down to test, it passed. It was wonderful.

The production guys saw me as a kid. They were all men and all much older than me. They liked the fact that I would come down and seek their advice. Of course, after they helped me once, I was like a stray cat that kept coming back to be fed.

My designs got much better, and in the next nine months, every one of the next three packets that I turned in worked. My boss told me, "Wow. I don't know what happened, but whatever you're doing, keep on doing it."

How did I keep the production guys helping me? I appreciated them. I thanked them. I bought them food—pizza, Chinese food, Indian food, cake, donuts. Most importantly, I'd bring them food when I had nothing testing in the lab. They stopped being the technicians to me. They started being "The Guys."

My reputation as a capable engineer was made. I did not change my method. I continued to work with the guys on the floor to understand what I was designing. I started bringing the mechanical guy who was working with me. I brought the wire harness guy down. Soon, we'd bring a whole team down, and we'd work with the production people to figure out what we were doing, and what we needed to do. It was amazing.

The Lesson

You have to pay attention to where your work is coming from and where your work is going. At a minimum, you need to go one level up and one level down to understand what's going on. To have an even better understanding, you could go two levels up and two levels down to see where the work is flowing.

No matter what you are doing, if you can involve the production people in your work, everyone improves. You are able to explain what you're doing and what you need, and they can tell you what they need. Communication does wonders. At every organization I've gone to, I ask, who is my customer and who am I a customer too? That understanding will serve you well.

Exercise: Chapter 11

Who in your organization is your customer and who are you a customer too?

Using your notebook, draw a small rectangle. On the left side of the rectangle, draw an arrow pointing in. On the right side, draw an arrow pointing out. Next, to the arrow pointing in, list the items that you expect to receive to do your job efficiently. Next, to the other arrow, list the outputs that are expected of you. Now, ruthlessly evaluate two things:

1. Are you receiving the things you need to be successful?
2. Are you providing the workflow needed for the company to be successful?

A deficiency in either of these areas will stop you from climbing the ladder of success. If you identify such a deficiency on either side of your input/output chart, take action to address the imbalance.

In the next chapter, let's discuss why researching a company before taking a job is a great idea. Changing positions is considered to be one of the top five stressors in a humans life by some psychologists. Let us see why it is worth it to take your time and do your research before changing positions.

Chapter 12
WTF?

"Don't wait until everything is just right. It will never be perfect. There will always be challenges, obstacles, and less than perfect conditions. So what. Get started now. With each step you take, you will grow stronger and stronger, more and more skilled, more and more self-confident, and more and more successful."
—Mark Victor

The Story

What the fuck?

I had just walked into my new office. I had taken a job as a Director at a large aerospace company, where the staff of eight businesses managers reported directly to me—320 people total. I was in charge of two facilities.

Before I explain the reaction I had when walking into my office that day, let me backtrack and say why I should have known there would be a problem.

This job found me. I had given a presentation at a conference about how building a team impacts inventory reduction. Afterward, an HR person walked up to me and asked for a copy of my resume, which I did not have. When I got home, I updated my resume and sent it to her.

They brought me in for an interview. It ended with them asking me to stay a second day to interview with the president of the company. That day, they made me an offer I could not refuse. We set the start date to be one month out, and the deal was done.

When I walked into my office on my first day, the previous Director's personal items were still there, and his seat was literally still warm. He had been walked out the same day I started.

I immediately had the secretary clean everything out. She packed it in a box and sent it to him. The guy deserved some dignity.

I called my first meeting with my new staff. There were a multitude of problems. Fortunately, I had seen these issues before. Over time, slowly but surely, we started making a dent in the problems. I was happy with that.

At the same time, I was somewhat unhappy at my boss's tendency to travel to my facility and take over my staff meetings. Since he was very Italian and somewhat hot-headed when things were not going the way he liked, he would not act very professionally.

The first sign that he was upset was that he would take off his jacket. If he continued to hear things he didn't like, he'd roll one sleeve up to his elbow, then the other. He would place his elbows on the table, put his head in his hands, and stare at us. We knew we were in trouble at that point.

Once he got to the point where he was certain things weren't going the way he wanted, he would begin to curse. It would be "fuck this" and "fuck that," "fuck you" and "fuck them" and "fuck everybody." After he had lost his temper and cursed everybody out for some time, he'd leave. I'd be left with the demoralized staff to figure out what to do next.

The fourth time he came to my facility to curse everybody out and leave, I decided I was no longer having it.

I had already met with him to asked him to not behave in that fashion. He had agreed, and then the very next week he came back and cursed out my staff again. I had to find another solution. What could I do? I worked for him—he did not work for me.

I decided that I was going to take control of the meeting. The next time he came to my building, sat down, and took off his coat, I rolled up my sleeves, put my head in my hands, and began to curse like a mother-fucking sailor.

I'm from Chicago, and I grew up on the rough side of town. I spent time as a teenager with pimps and whores. I spent the rest of the time in the ghetto. I knew how to curse someone out. For every fuck he said, I said four. When he got going, I said five to his one until he finally stopped cursing.

At last, we had a decent conversation about the numbers and went out about our business. I never had that problem with him again.

The Lesson

The moral to this story is that even though you work for someone, you are not helpless. You can't tell them what to do, but you can influence their behavior and gain control of the situation. It will take creative thinking, planning, and action.

A month later, he came up to me and said he appreciated that the meetings were going so much better. "I don't know what changed, but whatever you are doing, keep it up."

I responded with a simple, "Thank you, boss." I didn't say, "I got you to stop cursing everybody out."

When your boss is acting in a way that is hurting your team, you must act. If a conversation with your boss does not stop the behavior, then you must think of another way to make your point without antagonizing them. Remember, this is the person who will be evaluating you.

I took advantage of my boss's cultural values to make a point. It was worth the risk because his behavior was so disruptive and caused significant motivation problems with my team and within my facility. Solving this long-standing problem brought me leadership kudos and creativity points with those that were working directly for me.

Exercise: Chapter 12

Take a moment and identify two behaviors of your current boss that you would like to modify. In your workbook, record how you could address these behaviors in a constructive non-confrontational fashion.

Next, let's examine how to deal with situations when your friend is promoted to become your boss. The transition from being a peer to being a subordinate is tough on both the employee who is promoted and the employees who are left behind. It is even worse when the former friend turns out to be a terrible boss.

Chapter 13
Cheater

"From there to here and from here to there, funny things are everywhere."
—Dr. Seuss

The Story

This is about the time I helped myself get a really bad new boss.

I was working as a manufacturing manager for a Fortune 500 company. A new corporate vice president arrived. When he came in, he performed an organizational assessment and decided that we needed a new Director. This new Director would be promoted from inside the company. To be invited into the interview process, each candidate needed to provide a new productivity idea for the company. Then, during your interview, you would explain your idea further.

Four of us—me, the manager of facilities, the manager of design engineering, and the manager of new products—always ate lunch together, and we worked together to make the organization better. It had worked out well for all of us. The level of communication between divisions meant that we didn't have many glitches.

Three of the four of us admitted that we were going to try for the position. Each of us would have to work on our project independently so as not to share our ideas with other applicants. The fourth person in the group—the manager of design engineering—said he would not go after the position.

When the time came for them to announce who was going to get interviews, I found out that I had made it through. The person who said he didn't want to be the new Director also made it through. He had used a project that the four of us had worked on together and put it in for evaluation to get that interview.

You should have seen us reaching behind, trying to pull the knives out of our backs. He knifed us all pretty good. His project had input from everybody, while each of us had turned in projects that we had worked on alone.

I had an adverse reaction when I heard the news. The song "Smiling Faces Sometimes" by The Undisputed Truth immediately started playing in my mind.

Ultimately, he got the job. I had trouble not laughing around him. When he patted me on the back one day. I thought, *"I'm a-tellin' you, beware of the pat on the back. It just might hold you back"*.

He had been a great manager and friend, but he was a jerk boss. Since we'd all been hanging out together, he knew all the projects that were being completed in each of our departments. He used his knowledge in petty ways to show his old friends that he was the one in charge. Despite his jerky behavior, his former teammates (including me) did all we could to make him look good. It was a twist of the knife that he did not notice or appreciate our efforts to support his success.

The transition from having him as a peer to having him as a boss was hard. He turned into a jerk immediately. He never went out to lunch with us again, and he never called us on the phone individually. We had to set up times to see him on his schedule. I couldn't just walk by and stick my head in like I used to do. He even hired a jerk to fill his old position. Our group went from having no jerks to having a jerk we made plus one.

It did not get better at that company, so I left. When I did, I did not burn that bridge by telling him he was a jerk. I simply said that the transition had been unusually hard.

The Lesson

If you are competing for a position, don't believe anything anyone else says, especially if it's an open competition. Assume that every person is competing for the job. You want to keep it as fair as possible so that everyone has an equal chance. He cheated, won, and then acted badly. There was not a darn thing we could do about it.

Exercise: Chapter 13

How would you react if one of your current peers became your boss? Record the actions you could take to make the transition easier.

Take a moment and review your ambitions. Would you be comfortable in the position of being in charge of your friends and acquaintances? How would you manage the post-promotional relationships? Consider the actions you would take to insure your success and the success of your new team. Record in your workbook.

What happens when your new boss has been demoted into the position? What does it mean for you and your career? What action should you take to cover your butt? Next chapter, we will discuss this situation.

Chapter 14
Demoted Boss

"If you don't ask, the answer is always no."
—Nora Roberts

The Story

I was working away, minding my business, when our boss took another position. We inherited a boss who had been demoted, not by one position, but by two. You never want to work for a demoted boss. He will be so busy worrying about himself that he will not care about your career. Your paranoid boss will also move to protect himself from everyone else. This is not good for you.

Our new boss had been in charge of the entire engineering and maintenance departments. He oversaw hundreds of people with a huge budget. When he was demoted, he was assigned to run plant engineering—a small part of the engineering department. He now oversaw four people.

It was performance appraisal time, and the boss had a

plan to protect himself. His tactic was to give every single person a lousy performance review because if everybody working for him was terrible, he could not be replaced. This was terrible for the employees, but a great tactic for him, the boss. By the time my turn came, everyone knew what he was doing.

I sat across from him in his office while he busily tried to tell me why I was bad. I disagreed with everything he said. I wouldn't call the argument heated, but I would call it passionate. I was not going to take a bad performance review without a fight, even though I knew he wasn't going to change it.

In the midst of our conversation, he stood up, walked over, and stood over me while we talked about my review. I would not be intimidated by him, so I stood up too. In my heels, we were about the same height. We continued our passionate discussion with both of us standing well within each other's personal space.

After a few minutes, he walked back to his chair and sat down. I also sat.

I couldn't convince him to change the review. Although I rebutted it, it still went on record.

When the time came to sign the performance review, I didn't want to sign. He insisted that I did. At the bottom of the page, I wrote, "I disagree with this performance review. It is incorrect." The review was turned in with those words on it. Of course, the words didn't matter, but I felt better.

The Lesson

The lesson learned from this is that if your boss is demoted, run. Transfer if you can, quit if you need to, but get away from them *fast*. They will be scrambling to save their butts, and there is no time allocated for your career in that scenario.

Exercise: Chapter 14

If your boss was demoted, what three actions could you take immediately to protect your success? Think about what you can do, not what you can't do. Record in your workbook.

Now, consider what actions you can take long-term to address the situation.

Next up: Why is there an unwritten rule that tasks and activities be written down? Why should you insist that directions are provided in writing? In the next chapter, we will discover the importance of this simple rule.

Chapter 15
Get It in Writing

"None of us is as smart as all of us."
—Ken Blanchard

The Story

I was working in one of the northern states. It was cold. I hated it. The weather was horrific, and I fell in the snow at least three times one winter. I decided that, no, I was not going to stay in the snow anymore. My husband concurred. He believed that the economy was going to tank in our state shortly anyway.

I talked to my boss. At this time, I was a senior technical engineer. I let him know that I wanted to move to another position in another state. He laughed and said, "If you can get the company to move you, and it doesn't cost me anything. If you are willing to stay four weeks while I fill your position, I'm fine with you leaving." Then he took me out to lunch and gave me some tips on how to interview. I had worked on some challenging and exciting engineering problems under him and working with scientists had brought us success. He told me to use those accomplishments in any interview I got.

I managed to interview for a couple of jobs posted in a much warmer state. I was offered a position that required a high degree of technical skill and had a team with a less-than-stellar reputation. No one on the campus desired the job. Still, it was a promotion with a 25% raise, 8% of which was due to the higher cost of living. The package was excellent. It included moving expenses and spousal support so that my husband could find a job—sixty days worth of living expenses. I took the job.

They kept all their promises about moving costs and spousal support. But when I got my first paycheck, my base salary had only gone up 16%. I visited HR. "This is not the agreement that I had," I told them. "The agreement was that I would get a 25% raise because I moved for this position and nobody else wanted it." They said they would look into my file and see what the written agreement said.

I found out that the HR person I had been interfacing with had left the company. There were few written records of what we had discussed and no written paperwork that I had signed. I didn't recognize it when I took the job, but because I was transferring from one division to another, there should have been transfer paperwork. They told me that without this paperwork, I would have to live with the 16% raise; I would not get the 25%.

I recognized that I had made a critical error. Even if the HR person had not sent me any paperwork, I could have captured our agreements and sent them back to her for concurrence. That would have captured the information as well as prompted her to send me documentation.

I took HR's decision to my new boss, who said, "You don't have any paperwork. I can't support you in this." I then requested the issue be reviewed by the company arbitrator. The arbitrator said, "You don't have any documents. There is nothing we can do."

There was another problem associated with the job. When I arrived, neither the team I was taking over, nor my peers knew that I had been hired. The team had previously reported directly to my boss. I was installed as a middle manager without my boss informing the team. This led to all kinds of crazy speculation. One rumor was that I was the boss's girlfriend. He was single and had a reputation as a lady's man. He didn't hesitate to have affairs on campus. To dispel the theory, I made sure I invited my spouse to lunch with a few of my co-workers.

The third issue I ran into was that these guys didn't recognize that I had a shit-load of technical skills. I was a better engineer and designer than anyone else in my group. I had come from the technical innovation hub of the corporation, where I had worked with some of the best engineers in the world. But no one knew this, and on arriving, I had to prove that I had the technical skills needed to run the organization.

I accomplished this in a number of ways. I sat down and had decent one-on-ones with members of the team to show them that I understood what they were working on. I improved their designs and submitted them back to my team. I used my contacts back at my old position to assist me when I needed it.

The Lesson

The first takeaway is that you *must* get agreements in writing, even if you're transferring inside your own company. That lesson was tough.

The second lesson learned in this transfer was that you should insist on an introduction to your new team and peers. One of the things I ended up doing myself was writing my introduction paperwork saying, "Welcome, Toni Crowe, to the organization. She's coming from X, and she's providing Y, and she's taking over Z team." That information should have come from my boss. I waited too long to write it myself. If an arrival announcement has not come out within a week, you must do it. It took me about a month before I wrote and published mine.

The final lesson is to try not to work for jerks. I had a mature, older, experienced boss in the position I left. The new, young boss didn't have the savvy my previous boss had. Had I done a better investigation of my potential new boss, I could have made a more informed decision about taking the position. Do your homework. If I had done mine, I would have discovered that the location I was transferring to would not accept my lack of paperwork. I trusted that my new boss would take the appropriate actions to support me since that was what my old boss would have done. That assumption turned out to be wrong. My new boss did not help or defend me.

Have your paperwork, and make sure you get introduced. Do a good job researching who you will be working for, even if that person appears great at the interview.

Exercise: Chapter 15

If you are considering a move inside your organization, think about who you know in the area you are attempting to move to. Who would you contact? Who would you call to determine the culture and the situation in that part of the company? In your workbook, take a moment to record who you know outside your current assignment.

Once you do move, what activities should be completed before ten business days have passed in your new assignment? Record all in your notebook.

Next, we will review why it does not pay to overstep your boundaries with a new boss. Overstepping boundaries early in a relationship with the new boss causes career glitches.

Chapter 16
Don't Write Checks You Can't Cash

"Arrogance is used by the weak, while kindness is used by the strong."
—Hans F. Hansen

The Story

I was a new Director, working for a vice president who worked for the president. Their prior Director had passed away in a car accident, and the position had been open for a year before I filled it. The problem was that the team hadn't had a Director for so long that many of them had forgotten what their objectives were. A team without leadership reverts back to individuals doing the best they can for themselves. They deteriorate into chaos.

In particular, the facilities manager and his right-hand man had been doing whatever they wanted. They bent and broke the rules, but because the Director had died unexpectedly, the facilities manager was the next person who knew what was going on. The company had not taken him to task for his behavior.

When I came on board, I met with my entire team to discuss the fact that I was new and would be dependent on them for information. We had lost a year of time. If I decided to go in a direction that they disagreed with, they were welcome to come to my office and discuss it with me. I would listen and consider their input, but the final decision was mine. It was an excellent way to start our relationship since they had been leaderless for so long.

The facilities manager was running a project that I believed inappropriate. When I calculated the numbers, the return on investment (ROI) and the payback did not match the company guidelines. I asked him to terminate the project.

He told me, "Fine," and said that he would.

The next time I walked around, I found the project still running.

I asked him to shut it down a second time. Once again, he sat in my office and told me he would. His right-hand man was with him and agreed that they would take care of it.

When I went out to the factory two days later, the project was still going.

Fool me once, shame on you. Fool me twice, shame on me. When we had this conversation a third time, I asked the right-hand man to leave the room.

I spoke directly to the facility manager. "Listen," I said, "I'm not going to ask you again. You are going to turn that project off or you won't be in charge of it anymore."

He responded, "Who's going to run it?"

I smiled. "I will. You can't do my job, but I can do your job."

He took off his badge and arrogantly whipped it across my desk. It slid to a stop in front of me. "If you're going to take over my project, you don't need me. I'm just going to walk out the door."

It was a cool and decisive move. I suspected that he'd been pulling that stunt ever since the former Director left, forcing management to back down and let him do what he wanted. Unfortunately for him, I wasn't that management.

I sat straighter in my chair, picked up his badge, and put it in my pocket. "All right then, I understand. Pick your stuff up at your office, and I'll see you later."

His eyes got big. "Wait a minute, what are you saying?"

"You threw your badge on my desk. Paraphrasing your statement, you said, 'If I can't have it my way, I don't want to be here.' Well, you can't have your way. So, I'll see you later."

This was not the reaction he was expecting. "Well, maybe—"

I cut it. "There's no 'well maybe' in this. You threw your badge at me. Don't you have nine children? It looks like you'll be telling your wife, 'Hey honey, me and you and these nine kids aren't going be eating or living indoors much longer because I decided that I wanted to act like an arrogant ass with my boss. Guess what? My boss followed my lead and behaved like an arrogant ass with me.'" He sat there in silence, staring at me. "Go home," I said.

He left, but he did not go to HR on his way out of the

building. He took only his coat with him. I immediately notified security he was no longer allowed in the building. I did not tell them why. When he came to work the next morning, he couldn't enter. He kept working from the lobby, and anyone who wanted to see him had to meet him there. He found this humiliating since I had not notified anyone that I had fired him.

His wife called the next day and asked me, very nicely, to return his badge. She would personally guarantee that he would never whip it across my desk at me again. I told her that if he did, he would be fired for real. She again reassured me that he would not.

I let him return to work. During our "welcome back to work" conversation, I strongly notified him that I was not going to tolerate insubordination.

Don't write checks you can't cash.

The Lesson

The lesson here is quite simple: Don't pretend like you're going to do something that everyone knows you can't do. He had nine children. Work is not a hand of poker. You cannot bluff. When you do, someone will pick up that bluff and beat you with it like it's a two-by-four.

If you have intentions to leave the company or to make sure a particular project goes your way, don't back your boss into a corner. When he slid that badge across the desk to me, he gave me no option than to pick it up and put it in my pocket. I was the boss and I needed to behave that way.

Exercise: Chapter 16

In your workbook, identify at least one lose-lose situation that could occur in your current position? Write down the actions you should take to mitigate this situation occurring. Knowing what you could do and having a plan will add a level of calmness to any confrontation.

In the next chapter, we will review why it is important to keep the fact that you may be leaving to yourself. It is important to keep any and all information regarding changing positions out of your current workplace.

Chapter 17
Don't Tell Them You Are Leaving

"When you take risks you learn that there will be times when you succeed and times when you fail, and both are equally important."
—Ellen DeGeneres

The Story

I have a story that's not mine. It belongs to a family member, but it's one that we need to talk about. Although I never made this particular mistake, it was painful to watch someone else make it.

This family member had gotten a new job, and they were scheduled to start in five weeks. When I talked to them, I said, "Nope. Do not tell them that you are leaving. If you tell them, they are going to act ignorant."

They ignored my advice and told the company they were leaving a full month ahead of the time.

The company lost its mind. They were losing a precious asset who had been working successfully for them for several years. The company attempted to do two things. The first was to suck all the knowledge out of that asset's head. The second was to get that asset to do as much work as they possibly could before they left. As a result, there was nothing but trouble, trouble, and trouble. A person leaving an organization is not willing to work as hard as a person who is staying. Comparatively, the company is willing to put tremendous heat on the person leaving because there is nothing they can do about it. What would they do? Quit? No. They have already given notice.

The company made this person's life miserable until they left the organization, but it was an unnecessary ordeal.

When leaving a company, the rules are clear and simple. If they behave badly when employees leave give them one week's notice and be prepared for them to walk you out the door the moment you tell them that you're leaving. If they do, depending on which state you are in, they must give you one week's pay. If they don't behave badly when employees leave, provide them with the standard two weeks' notice, but again, be prepared to have them walk you out the door. Depending on the state, they will still have to give you two weeks' pay.

Bad behavior is when employees give notice and they are walked out immediately or for the next two weeks, they are given work that is the equivalent of cleaning restrooms.

The Lesson

The moment you tell a company you're leaving, you are no longer that company's asset, and they begin to treat you as such. Make sure that you don't violate this simple rule as you change jobs.

Exercise: Chapter 17

Write in your workbook

"I will sell no wine—no wait. Write in your workbook, "I will not give any more notice when I am leaving than is necessary".

Up next: There is a reason you want balance in your life. Working all the time is not a good place to be to find happiness on this earth.

Chapter 18
Dead or Alive

"We cannot change the inevitable. The only thing we can do is play on the one string we have, and that is our attitude… I am convinced that life is 10% what happens to me and 90% how I react to it. And so, it is with you… we are in charge of our attitudes."
—Charles R. Swindoll

The Story

I was working as the manager of manufacturing engineering when we found one of our employee's dead on the toilet at the end of the day.

The entire situation was incredibly disturbing. The employee, who I'll call Joe, had been a workaholic. He had been married four times and divorced four times. He freely admitted that one of the issues in all of his marriages was his enthusiasm for his job. Joe was at work seven days a week, ten hours a day. His boss liked to brag that he could do the work of two people, and he did. He was always there. I don't believe there was ever a time when I came to work, and he was not there.

I attended Joe's funeral and wake. I was the only person from our company to visit, and I was glad that no one else had come. The funeral parlor was empty. Two or three people were loitering around. The man had no friends or family to speak of.

The company replaced him in two weeks.

The Lesson

Joe's death taught me to care more about things outside of work than those at work. When I am at work, I give it my all. I am as productive as I can be, and I use every tool in my toolbox to make the environment better for my company. But when it is time to leave, I go home. I might work long hours for a number of weeks, but I make it my business to be there for every critical activity my family needs me for. I will even leave work in the middle of my long day to support those I love. So should you.

Exercise Chapter 18

In your workbook, draw three columns. Label them "Work," "Home," and "Comment." Above these, record the percentage of time you believe is required at home for a healthy work-life balance. Calculate these percentages against a twenty-four-hour clock. Twelve hours of work in a day is 50%.

For the next two weeks, record how much time you spend at work and home. Include commuting time in the work hours. Include time spent dropping your children off at school and running errands during the day as home time.

At the end of two weeks, calculate the percentages. How does the percentage for home hours compare to the portion you determined was required for work-life balance? If the percentage is plus or minus 5% in either direction, then you have a decision to make. You can adjust your life to match your desires, or you can leave the imbalance in place. Each must determine their work-life balance.

The next chapter is not about corporate America, but it contains a lesson that is invaluable for success in any organization.

Chapter 19
Treachery

"For there to be betrayal, there would have to have been trust first."
—Suzanne Collins, *The Hunger Games*

The Story

One of the most treacherous jobs I ever had was when I was in a Welfare-to-Work program in Chicago, Illinois.

I was training to become a certified lab assistant while being paid by the state of Illinois. Each morning, I was due to work at 5 a.m. From 5 a.m. to 8:30 a.m., the hospital trained us to be phlebotomists. Our instructors were the leaders in the lab. We wore white shoes, white stockings, white sweaters, and little white hats. Our job was to collect specimens of various bodily fluids (blood, feces, skin, throat in the mornings' swabs, etc.) from the hospitalized patients in the mornings from five a.m. until nine a.m. then attend class and lab training in the afternoon. The last two hours of our ten-hour days were in practical experience, working beside the laboratory technicians. There was lots of competition for this position because the hospital had only one job available at the end of our training. There were twelve of us—ten African-Americans, one Asian, and one white person. Throughout our training the Asian, the white girl, and I were always at the top of the class. The teacher would line the papers up and pass them out in grade order. I did not appreciate getting my paper second or third. I wanted to receive my paper first. If there was more than one 100%, the teacher would call us up together to receive the papers. If you had 99%, you were second. I disliked being second.

We were trained in hematology, microbiology, biology, and human physiology. We had training in all the practical aspects of the lab as well. We learned how to utilize the test equipment, how to measure things, and how to work with very sick patients. At the end of our training, we would take a test. The state of Illinois administered the test so that we could become certified laboratory assistants (CLA).

When the test results came back, I had the highest score ever recorded in the history of the class. I also had one of the best techniques for phlebotomy and technical lab measurements. I assumed I would get the job. I had forgotten something important—or rather, something I probably never knew having grown up on the south side of Chicago.

This competition was not fair. When the time came to award the job, the position went to the white girl. Since the entire lab was white, I had always known there was a possibility that I would not get the job. I assumed that because of my test results, there was no way to go around me. I was wrong.

When I went to the hospital administrator's office to discuss why I did not get the position, there was a new criterion in place. The reason I did not get the job was that the white girl had much better "soft skills" than I did. This was interesting, since "soft skills" had never been mentioned as a criterion for the job. We had never been taught soft skills nor had we practiced soft skills. The first time I heard of "soft skills" was sitting in the office with the two teachers and the administrator. When I tried to understand what these "soft skills" were, they could not explain them to me. The best I understood was that they were the way you interfaced with everyone around you. It was an immeasurable magic thing that you either had or you didn't. I didn't have it, and she did. This was a stunning development. I was devastated.

The Lesson

The lessons here were doubly hurtful since I was young and had worked so hard.

The first is to understand exactly what the requirements are for anything you are seeking. These cannot be delivered verbally. They must be written down where everyone can see them and agreed upon before any action is taken. The requirements for the job should be clearly stated so that there are no hidden "soft requirements." The problem with soft requirements is that they are entirely subjective and are different in each person's mind.

The second lesson is to double-check your actual status and make sure it is the status you believe you have. At no point during the class did either teacher promise me that job, but I understood the implications were always that I would get it. The bottom line is that I never sought reassurance that I was doing all the things needed to have the position come my way. As such, there was no acknowledgment that I was even in the running for the position.

The last lesson was that not getting the position at the hospital was the best thing that could have happened to me. Instead, I found a better paying job at the private hospital across the street. It was here that I started learning and understanding the rewards of leadership. I met two individuals who would be instrumental in my return to college. This leads us back to a simple claim that all things happen for a reason.

Exercise: Chapter 19

Research the written job description for your next promotion. Capture in your workbook.

Introduce yourself to the person currently holding that position to gain an understanding of the any hidden skills required for that position. Capture your findings in your workbook.

Record three actions you will take to address expertise needed both written and hidden.

Next, we will review why you must gain your understanding of all documents handed out by your company. There is the potential for misunderstandings if you proceed with one understanding while the company has a different mentality.

Chapter 20
Read and Understand the Contract

"Tricks and treachery are the practice of fools, that don't have brains enough to be honest."
—Benjamin Franklin

The Story

A friend of mine was working at a medical products company as an engineering specialist. The organization was a dream company, one of those touchy-freely, California-type companies that did everything they could to keep the employees happy. That was before it was bought. The new owner had an entirely different idea of how the company should be run.

One of the things he changed was the culture of employee ownership in the company. He made it very clear that he was in charge. Early on, he invited all the employees from one department—about twenty people altogether—to bring their spouses to a special dinner. At this dinner, a new project was introduced. It would require tremendous sacrifice from the employees for the company to get the product out on time. The promise was made that if successful, employees and their spouses could take a vacation trip to Hawaii at the company's expense.

The company gave each employee a contract to make it clear that they were serious about the Hawaiian trip. The team scuffled and sacrificed for eighteen months to complete the project. It was done on time and on the budget. But, even though they had contracts from the company, the team did not go to Hawaii.

It turned out that the contract had a clause in it that said the assessment of the contract's successful execution was at the total discretion of the owner. There were no parameters around the decision-making process. The owner decided that, even though the project was completed successfully, the team had not performed to his satisfaction.

There was no Hawaii trip. Instead, after eighteen months, each person got a check for about $400. My friend transferred out of the group.

The two groups that did go to Hawaii were the senior management team and the sales team that won the contract. The owner felt that those individuals had performed to his satisfaction. While they watched Jay Leno perform for the senior managers and the sales associates in Hawaii, the technical team sat at home working. As if to rub it in, the meeting was televised from Hawaii to the entire company.

The Lesson

Anytime a company puts something in writing for their employees; the employees need to understand the contents of the document. How is success defined for the project? How will it be determined that the goals of the project are met? What are the timelines? What are the parameters? What's the payout, and when will you get the payout for achieving the goals?

Employees can't trust documents that are handed to them without having the documents reviewed. The contract may contain a clause that makes it null and void no matter what they do. That is a useless contract. In this story, the success of the team was based on one person's uninformed opinion of the team's success. When the assessor is not a part of the team, the result is seldom fair. My friend never accepted a contract again from anyone without having it thoroughly reviewed.

Excerise Chapter 20

In your workbook record for every project that you are working on.

1. How is success defined for the project, how will it be determined that the goals of the project have been met?
2. What are the agreed upon timelines?
3. What are the success parameters?
4. What is the payout?

In the next chapter, let's compile all of the practical issues we have addressed to see how they play together.

Chapter 21
Putting It All to Use

"Even if you are on the right track, you'll get run over if you just sit there."
—Will Rogers

All the tips in this book are things that I wish someone had told me when I was trying to be promoted. None of them is a silver bullet, but together they will give you the opportunity to do very well in the corporate world. Use the advice here to leap over your competition.

As I mentioned earlier, I had a colleague who died on the toilet at work. We found him at the end of the day when the cleaning crew came through. I was still there when they zipped him up in a black plastic bag and carried him away. Within two days, a temporary production manager was in place. In two weeks, the permanent replacement was on the floor working. My late colleague's desk had been cleaned out. His overstuffed file cabinet containing twenty-six years of work was gone. A new chair was put into his office. It was as if he was never there. The corporation replaced him without blinking an eye.

Don't let your work swallow you like it did this man, but still do the things you need to reach your definition of success. If that definition includes climbing the corporate ladder, use this book as a practical primer to avoid traps and mistakes.

If you have used this book with a friend or group, keep the conversations prompted by the exercises going. Just because you've finished reading doesn't mean you've stopped learning and figuring out how to make things better.

In the corporate world, many things are not as they seem. Bosses may appear all-powerful, but they are not. Bosses are employed by their corporations to meet goals and objectives. They are tools to be used to meet the objectives of the shareholders, not the objectives of their subordinates. Your boss is not your friend. He hired you because you have skills and expertise that are needed to meet his goals. Like a bullet, the leader has been hired to seek out targets and destroy them. Anything or anyone blocking that target will be hit as the bullet drives for the center. It is not personal; it *is* business.

As one climbs up corporate chain, the decisions required to effect more people, more money and more capital. After a certain point, the day to day decisions are so big; those decisions are no longer publicly shared. The position becomes more isolated, with fewer and fewer others are allowed into the decision-making process. For those very tough complicated decisions where there is no right answer, the boss will often seek counsel from his team and other leaders but make the decision alone.

When making life-altering decisions in my career, friendship was never one of my considerations. I never considered the number of friends I knew in a company as a driver. Money, power, challenge, location, pay, benefits, bonuses and the ability to affect the organization and company reputation would be considered. Like a bullet, I was hired and then launched toward a target with specific instructions on what to hit. Anything in my way was going to be dealt with.

Management problems will occur. *Bullets and Bosses Don't Have Friends* will keep you a step ahead of the most common problems in corporate America. If you are ambitious, have what it takes to be a leader, and can get an edge, then you can succeed. This book has provided you with some of the most common situations that occur with bad bosses. Use it to hone your edge and be prepared when they come but always remember: **Bullets and Bosses Don't Have Friends**.

Bonus Material

Book 1 Chapter 1
"Never A $7 Wh*re"

A Thrilling Bootstrap Success Story About Determination in the Face of Overwhelming Odds (The $7 Series Book 1)

Chapter 1
Introduction

The simplest fact of life is that every person in the world makes mistakes.

But no mistake needs to be unrecoverable. No person deserves to have their life pushed off track by one poor decision, their entire life affected by one single moment.

The second simplest fact of life is that most people never rebound from what they perceive as a "fatal" mistake.

But it doesn't have to be that way.

There are ways to recover from seemingly fatal mistakes. This book details one such mistake I made and the techniques that I used to recover my life and to make a difference in my family's and my descendants' success.

At just eighteen years old, I ran away with the love of my life. I fled from Chicago, Illinois, to Cleveland, Ohio, against the advice of my mother, father, friends—even my enemies. I left my three-year-old son with my mom to pursue a career as a glamorous model. It turned out the man was a pimp, and my fellow models-to-be were prostitutes. I was slated to be the newest addition to the brothel.

We all make mistakes, and that was my own. Seemingly fatal, yes?

Instead, thirty years later, after having developed a series of techniques to change my thinking and deal with my bad decision head-on, I am now ready to comfortably retire as an Operations Vice President having worked at some of the top Fortune 50 companies in the US and UK.

Even now I recall how my past is a stark contrast from the life I achieved.

"I will never be a seven-dollar whore."

The words echoed in my mind as I sat back in the soft leather seat of a limousine. My driver, ever attentive, asked if I needed anything. I told him that I didn't as I sipped my smart water. I wasn't going to tell him we were riding past the very hotel where I had stood up to Baby.

I was in Cleveland to negotiate a new maintenance contract with our Japanese partners, a seventy-million-dollar deal. The driver had picked me up at the airport. He had a salad from Guarino's and ice-cold water waiting for me. I sipped my water slowly, picked at my salad, and thought again about Baby.

I remembered being in the lobby of the hotel. I was being trained as a "paid companion." That particular night I was assigned to observe the ladies as they went on their dates, collect the money when they came downstairs to prep for their next date, and then dispatch cleaners to the rooms to prepare them for the next encounter. All three ladies I was responsible for were having a busy night, so it was difficult to keep track of everything.

I had no idea if Prince, the pimp, was watching me or not. I had no idea, but I was on my toes in case he was. I was taking my instructions from Baby, who was in charge that night. I was dressed in a black suit, hair pinned up, beautifully sensible shoes, and a matching purse. Small diamond earrings accented my dark brown eyes. Baby came down and sat next to me. She informed me that I needed to come to the room with her.

"No," I told her. "I'm collecting the money."

Prince had not forced me to prostitute myself . . . yet. I was to dispatch and hold the money. If the ladies were arrested, any money on them would be confiscated.

Prince was busy with one of the other girls, so Baby discreetly grabbed my arm and squeezed. We didn't want to attract attention. "Tee, you will do what I tell you. I'm the one in charge."

Baby had successfully cowed me on many occasions, but not today. I continued to protest. "No, I'm not your whore."

Baby leaned in close to me. "You are whatever I say you are. You are my whore. You will do what I say. I'll charge what I want for you, tonight. A thousand, five hundred, fifty, or even seven." Baby laughed. "You'll be my seven-dollar whore."

I reached out and put my hand on Baby's arm and squeezed her hard. "I'm not your seven-dollar whore. I'm not the same girl who came here two months ago. I'm not that bitch. I'm the brand-new bitch you made me into. I will mess you up right here, right now, if you don't let me go. I'm not going upstairs."

We stared into each other's eyes.

"I will never be a seven-dollar whore. Never." I said it with such force that spittle came out of my mouth and landed on her cheek.

Baby wiped it off and let go of my arm. "I'm going to fuck you up," she said.

I laughed. "You are going to fuck me up more than I have fucked myself up?" I laughed again, bitterly. "That might be hard to do." I sat down and took a deep breath as she walked back to the elevator. Tears filled my eyes, but I didn't let them fall. This was all my fault.

The car stopped moving, and I snapped out of my reminiscing. I thought about how blessed I was. I was respected in my company, one of the high-potential players. I had a decent career, a beautiful family, and a devoted husband who knew all about my wild years and did not care. He kept urging me to write a book about it.

As I walked into the skyscraper, I thought about how strange it was to be back in Cleveland. What would I be doing now if I had not had the smarts to escape? Would I even be alive? I had been lucky in many ways. I had been very dumb in others. Perhaps my husband was right. When I had time, once the kids were grown, maybe I should write a book about my wild times.

This is that book.

People often lead poor lives because they cannot find a way out of their self-made binds. They have no hope. They see no future. But I am here to say that there is always hope, always a possibility of a bright future. I have helped a number of people in desperate circumstances, especially women, change their thinking and find success despite their situations. I tell them my story and how I escaped my destiny.

I give myself as an example. No mistake or circumstance is escape proof.

There is no inescapable future.

An old Chinese proverb says, "A journey of a thousand miles begins with a single step."

Once you gain an understanding of how I escaped my fate, you will never be at the mercy of destiny again. You will be in control of your life. Your past mistakes will not define you or your future. You will identify and escape showstopper, life-changing decisions before becoming embroiled in them. You will kick existing bad decisions and habits to the curb. You will become so good at identifying and stopping these behaviors that I hope you will share this book, or even just portions of it, with others who need similar help.

Become the one who does good and spreads kindness to others by helping them make a second destiny for themselves.

Don't allow anyone to take your future away from you. No matter how mired in rottenness, or boredom, or plain bad activities you have become, your strength and power can take you out of that mindset and set you free. Set your future free.

Get out of the physical and mental mindset holding you back.

If doesn't matter where you are now—use my narrative to give yourself hope and make your life better. If I can do it, anyone can.

Once again: A journey of a thousand miles begins with a single step.

So take that step, turn the page, and let us begin my story.

Did you enjoy this excerpt?
If so, buy the book at Amazon.com
https://www.amazon.com/dp/b07g5q2gv5

It Couldn't Be Done

Somebody said that it couldn't be done,
    But he with a chuckle replied
That "maybe it couldn't," but he would be one
    Who wouldn't say so till he'd tried.
So he buckled right in with the trace of a grin
    On his face. If he worried he hid it.
He started to sing as he tackled the thing
    That couldn't be done, and he did it.
Somebody scoffed: "Oh, you'll never do that;
    At least no one ever has done it";
But he took off his coat and he took off his hat,
    And the first thing we knew he'd begun it.
With a lift of his chin and a bit of a grin,
    Without any doubting or quiddit,
He started to sing as he tackled the thing
    That couldn't be done, and he did it.
There are thousands to tell you it cannot be done,
    There are thousands to prophesy failure;
There are thousands to point out to you one by one,
    The dangers that wait to assail you.
But just buckle in with a bit of a grin,

Edgar Guest, 1881–1959

ACKNOWLEDGMENTS

Since he found out many years ago that I love to write (and that I ran away with a pimp!), my husband Bill has been urging me to write my story down. It became a running joke in our family, including with my children, Sean and Tamara. "Mom," they would ask, "when are you going to write the 'I could have been a $7 whore' story?" I would smile and tell them, "Someday." Recently, Bill pointed out that I had both an unusual university experience and corporate career as well. I, of course, continued to talk about "someday." Well, someday for one book has expanded into someday for four books and two short reads.

My big dysfunctional family continues to surprise me with their unyielding support.

And finally, my technical support and spouse. I would never have written this book b(or any other without you. The support you provide remains priceless, your unwavering belief in me makes all things possible.

I love you all and I could never have done this without you.

Thank you so much for buying and reading the third

book in the $7 series—*Bullets and Bosses Don't Have Friends, My Journey from a Lady of the Night to the Lady of the Boardroom Part 3* You could have spent your time doing anything else, but you chose to read my book. I am very pleased and grateful that you did.

If you missed the first two books in the $7 series, Book 1 Never a $7 Whore, and Book 2 The Daytime Lives of the Ladies of the Night, I invite you to go back and read them, I have had a most interesting life full of ups and downs that others can easily learn from.

To buy the books: http://tonicrowewriter.com

If you enjoyed my book (or if you didn't), I would like to hear from you on my website.

I am a new writer; **it would help me immensely if you write an honest review** at Amazon.com. . Simply click on the review area next to the stars and start your book review there.

> Thank you for your feedback. Your feedback helps me improve my writing. I hope you have a great day.

–Toni Crowe, The Writer

See http://tonicrowewriter.com for the latest news on the fifth book in the series, "From Zero to Family Hero, How to Get a Degree When You Don't Know Anything." Coming soon.

The fifth book details the fascinating struggle Toni had attended the University of Illinois to obtain her Engineering degree. She *was the first in her mother's family to complete college. Her lack of knowledge about the college experience was stunning. She graduated with a degree in Electrical Engineering from the University of Illinois, Chicago.*

Appendix A
Citations

1.
Duck Soup
Release date: November 17, 1933 (USA)
Director: Leo McCarey
Production company: Paramount Pictures
Producer: Herman J. Mankiewicz
Screenplay: Harry Ruby, Bert Kalmar, Arthur Sheekman, Nat Perrin

Appendix B
Promotion and Training Path

My Career Path

Associate Engineer > Engineer > Senior Engineer > Principle Engineer > Production Supervisor > Wire Harness Manager> Purchasing Manager> Production Manager> Manufacturing Engineering Manager> Design Engineering Manager > Director> Site Leader, Integrated Supply Chain Director > President> Vice President> Director> Vice President.>CEO

My Training Path

Medical Assistant (MA) > Certified Laboratory Assistant (CLA) > Bachelors Degree: Engineering (BSEE>) Engineer In Training (EIT) > Masters of Organizational Management (MOM)> Professional Engineer (PE)> Certified Manager (CM),> Six Sigma Green Belt> Six Sigma Black Belt>Japanese Productivity Study Group

Appendix C.
Quotes

"The road to success and the road to failure are almost exactly the same."—Colin R. Davis

"This is a tough place for a woman. I've been put down, pushed aside, knocked out. Truth is I have had to fight my whole life because of who I am, who I love, and where I started. But I didn't let anything get in my way."— Sharice Davis

"To succeed in life, you need two things: ignorance and confidence." —Mark Twain

"Don't be distracted by criticism. Remember—the only taste of success some people have is when they take a bite out of you."—Zig Ziglar

"Bosses shape how people spend their days and whether they experience joy or despair, perform well or badly or are healthy or sick. Unfortunately, there are hoards of mediocre and downright rotten bosses out there, and the big gaps between the best and the worst." —Robert L. Sutton, *Good Boos, Bad Boss: How to Be the Best… and Learn from the Worst*

"Unless someone like you cares a whole awful lot, it's not going to get better. It's not." —Dr. Seuss

"To be a champion, I think you have to see the big picture. It's not about winning and losing; it's about the everyday hard work and about thriving on a challenge. It's about embracing the pain that you'll experience at the end of a race and not being afraid. I think people think too hard and get afraid of a certain challenge." —Summer Sanders

"The secret to success is to know something that nobody else knows."—Aristotle Onasis

"Success is not final; failure is not fatal: it is the courage to continue that counts."—Winston Churchill

"Nearly all men can stand adversity, but if you want to test a man's character, give him power."—Abraham Lincoln

"Don't live down to expectations. Go out there and do something."— Wendy Wasserstein

"Don't wait until everything is just right. It will never be perfect. There will always be challenges, obstacles, and less than perfect conditions. So what. Get started now. With each step you take, you will grow stronger and stronger, more and more skilled, more and more self-confident, and more and more successful." —Mark Victor

"From there to here and from here to there, funny things are everywhere."—Dr. Seuss

"None of us is as smart as all of us."—Ken Blanchard

"If you don't ask, the answer is always no." —Nora Roberts

"Arrogance is used by the weak, while kindness is used by the strong." —Hans F. Hansen

"When you take risks you learn that there will be times when you succeed and times when you fail, and both are equally important." —Ellen DeGeneres

"We cannot change the inevitable. The only thing we can do is play on the one string we have, and that is our attitude… I am convinced that life is 10% what happens to me and 90% how I react to it. And so it is with you… we are in charge of our attitudes." —Charles R. Swindoll

"For there to be betrayal, there would have to have been trust first."—Suzanne Collins, *The Hunger Games*

"Tricks and treachery are the practice of fools, that don't have brains enough to be honest." —Benjamin Franklin

"Even if you are on the right track, you will get run over if you just sit there." —Will Rogers

Other books by Toni Crowe, The Writer

Never a $7 Wh*re is a heartfelt memoir that will light a fire in your soul. She was a would-be teenage prostitute. Now she's a Fortune Fifty VP.

Buy at Amazon.com
Kindle, Audiobook, Paperback

https://www.amazon.com/dp/B07G5Q2GV5

Have you ever wondered: "What do the women who sell their bodies and souls at night do in the daytime"?

Buy at Amazon.com

Kindle, Audiobook, Paperback

https://www.amazon.com/dp/B07GT9KYZK

The workbook for "Bullets and Bosses Don't Have Friends" contains practical lessons and a set of exercises for each chapter that you can apply to your career.

Buy at Amazon.com

Kindle, Audiobook, Paperback

https://www.amazon.com/dp/B07JGT23V6

ABOUT THE AUTHOR

Toni Toni Crowe is an award-winning and accomplished executive with 30 years of experience as a CEO/President, Vice-President, Director, Engineer, and Manager across multiple sectors including high tech, consumer and nuclear sensors, Aerospace, film production and glass. She has extensive experience in P&L, Manufacturing, Operations Management, and Lean. She has participated in a number of mergers and acquisitions. Toni is currently the President and CEO of **Just One:** her company which is dedicated to changing lives, one life at a time.

Toni can be contacted at-
https://www.tonicrowewriter.com/

www.ingramcontent.com/pod-product-compliance
Lightning Source LLC
LaVergne TN
LVHW022323080426
835508LV00041B/2169